THE PSALMS OF JOEL

Volume III

By: JOEL W. ADDISON, JR

PublishAmerica
Baltimore

First printing

Unless otherwise indicated, Bible quotations are taken from NKJ version.

PublishAmerica has allowed this work to remain exactly as the author intended, verbatim, without editorial input.

ISBN: 978-1-4489-6121-4
PUBLISHED BY PUBLISHAMERICA, LLLP
www.publishamerica.com
Baltimore

Printed in the United States of America

LYRICS OF LILACS

Wild flowers bloom in the hardest places
Like Columbine 'atop Rocky Mount'
Helen's a ray of hope to the broken
Yea, for the thirsty, she springs afount'
    Her disabled are not discarded
    Nor told, "they are of no use,"
    But words of restoration
    New skills and trades to unloose.
The depth of her sweet nature
God's Comforter has bestowed
Blessing the lives around her
How unselfishly it flows.
    When others have lost the song they had
    And the smell of their soul's grown stale
    The Lifter of Helen's head shall sing,
    "Glory to God! Lift that veil."
Encouragement has become a dead art
Only to gain man's favor
Yet, when it's done to please our Lord
Good results will never waiver.
    At Ravensbrooke Elijah was fed
    But who did he have to give thanks?
    Only the "One" who made the Raven,
    The rivers and the banks.
I thank God for but a glimpse
Of His pure love I see in Helen
For she's given those reins of her life to Him
A precious vessel her Captain may sail in.
    God release that same unfettered
    Love to serve in me
    Blessing and being that flower
    As Helen is, happily!

MOM'S THANKSGIVING PRAYER

Father God I thank you
From this hospital bed
Frustrated yet not bitter
In chronic pain though not dead.
   Will I be healed
    Or bravely suffer
    Is it being selfish
    To ask that I not recover?
I'm tired and this fight
has worn me thin
Then all of a sudden
Another battle again.
    God of all mercies
    I know you are there
    These drugs so confuse me
    I just wonder where.
My vision's blurred and speech is slurred
Yet my mind is still intact
I question though each moment
How my body may choose to react.
    It's a month before Christmas
    Not a single card have I written
    I'm concerned and would like to write
    But my coordination's a little smitten.
My family's been great
I don't want to bother
Can't you release me
To go home to you, Father?
    What work is left unfinished
    May I clock in and get it done?
    If there's a reconciliation left
    Please let your counsel come.

gressmen, Senators, hear our plea,
oid the judgment of God's decree…
hat, if My people, who are called by My Name
ll NOT repent of their evil game,
land shall I smite with a terrible plight
wiftly as, a thief in the night!" "
do justly, love mercy, and walk humbly with thy God
ll I required of you,
injustice and hatred and pride you have sought
arrogance to do!
banks and businesses
e credited away
nce firm economy
ger shall it stay!
humanist ideology
your schools you've preached
interest paid on what they've said
emon foe's unleashed…
n with no respect
ng they know it all
nal ethics
y shall fall!
help us in these last few days
re our Savoir comes
heed His call and give our all
Heaven's eternally our home.

I am truly thankful
That you've heard my prayer
And you're not caught in some cloud jam
Way up in Heaven somewhere.
   I'm content with grace
   You've given me to survive
   And that you "ARE" concerned
   Whether I'm dead or alive
May your Peace inhabit
My soul's ever being
Until it is you, Dear Lord
That I will be seeing.

Now, Dear Lord, I'm home with you
Flying on wings of the wind
Rejoicing with no pain nor sorrow
No past failures to ever amend.
   O' grave where is thy victory
   O' death where is thy sting?
   Thou canst not hound this mortal shell
   For I reside now with My King!

"RESCUE PSALM 911"

He who dwells in the secret place
Sheltered and covered by the Most High
Will say of the Lord, "you're my Refuge
In whom I can trust to get by…
    From deadly disease you'll protect me
    A shield of faithfulness you bear
    From terror of night or arrows in flight
    Evil stalkers and plagues beware!"
A thousand to ten at my right hand
But never to me shall they come
If God continues my habitat
Punishment only shall I see of the wicked one!
    Disaster and harm will not come near
    For His angels shall guard my way
    Soaring to lift me into their hands
    Kept above the demonic fray.
"Because he loves Me," says the Lord,
"I will rescue him;
Protecting, for he acknowledges my Name
Despite the trouble or how grim.
    I'll deliver him with honor
    Giving long life to satisfy
    Showing him My salvation
    For him on the cross I died."

"A TRAGEDY IN OUR LAN

We the people, in order to form,
A more perfect Union thought:
That all men were created equal,
Until the unborn question was brought!
    Should our special inalienable rights
    Be presented by "those" who can't fight?
Who'll defend the little ones
Whose deaths are 20 times those done by guns?
    God gave us life, liberty and a quest
    To fulfill our goals of happiness.
Yet we, in our pride, began our demise
By shedding the blood of innocent lives.
    God spared not His own nation of Israel
    When sacrificed children's blood was to spil
Our land shall be given to those we hate
Because our unrepented sins are great!
The fear of A.I.D.S. and other such plagues
    Are broadcast on the news
    Through liberal, anything goes, reporters
    That scorn the conservatives' views!
Mockeries of Jesus Christ
And child pornography
Are among the list of tactical weapons
Destroying our society.
    Our worship of eye—do$$ar-TREE
    Is passed on by an addiction to: T.V.
Sex, violence, murder, and theft
Are telling our children, "there's nothing left
    Of morals and integrity"
    Just "Be All that you can Be!"
God gives us grace that we may stand
Above the decadence of our land!
    Help us to be strong and shout our voice
    That such lewdness is NOT our choice!

SHS '72

From Kent State on through Watergate
Cambodia and Vietnam,
The Beatles, Hendrix, and flower power,
Uncertainty filled our land.

But fresh from school we embarked,
A chartered course for some,
Invigorated to mold our future
Completing what our parents hadn't done.

College, careers, and misguided ventures
Brought questions we'd never had
'Cause now they are asking us
You know, High School wasn't all that bad.

Why, the kids need help and there's bills to pay
I don't think two jobs are enough.
I need a degree to get a raise
No more is the option of giving up.

It seems my parents kind of depend on me
I feel the drawing of that obligation
From all the years of tears I brought 'em
To a glaring indication...

How math, English and history
Weren't exactly meant to equip me
Yet passing them and other test
Would get me ready to do my best...

Of accomplishing goals that really matter
Not pipe dreams that just wash and splatter
Against the walls of adversity
Blinded by what I couldn't see.

This strength of character and patience brought
Traits that I earlier might have fought.
For respect and authority they often resembled
Yes, they're earned, NOT owed and my pride has been humbled.

A good family and name are cause enough
To put up now with my two boys' stuff.
I raised Cain in school and could have done better
But to raise "My" kids, I'm a dedicated debtor!

"ICE BOX CHRISTIANS"

"What's for dinner? Well, let me see
Seems like some 'good' leftovers."
A drumstick here some macaroni
I'll give the rest to Rover.
    We as covenant people,
    Albeit by god's Grace,
    Don't even give our brother food
    Despite his starved sunken face.
The Bread of Life gave from His table
A measure prepared for the Jews
Yet, drawn by the faith of a Gentile mom
'The Cafeteria' was open for her to choose
    We worry about our spiritual diet
    While others starve to death
    Or if their problems crave toward us
    We glibly say, "There's nothing left."
Are we like Pharisees so callous with our faith
So long as our family's fed and safe, no more can we relate?
    Is our tradition more important
    Than that which God commands…
    To love our brother as ourselves
    Hasn't been the attitude of our land
We're guilty church! Wake up!
We are the moral guide
Whether the court rules God's TEN LAWS
Are left in our outside.
    Little boys need big brothers
    And weekend fathers too
    But our high profile with society
    Leaves a wisp of time for use.
Your business nor your busy-ness
Won't impress God at all

When He's impressed you to help someone
More than a random call.
    As much as you have done it
    Unto the least of these
    My brethren you have done it
    Not to them but Me. Jesus the King!

I am truly thankful
That you've heard my prayer
And you're not caught in some cloud jam
Way up in Heaven somewhere.
    I'm content with grace
    You've given me to survive
    And that you "ARE" concerned
    Whether I'm dead or alive
May your Peace inhabit
My soul's ever being
Until it is you, Dear Lord
That I will be seeing.

Now, Dear Lord, I'm home with you
Flying on wings of the wind
Rejoicing with no pain nor sorrow
No past failures to ever amend.
    O' grave where is thy victory
    O' death where is thy sting?
    Thou canst not hound this mortal shell
    For I reside now with My King!

"RESCUE PSALM 911"

He who dwells in the secret place
Sheltered and covered by the Most High
Will say of the Lord, "you're my Refuge
In whom I can trust to get by…
    From deadly disease you'll protect me
    A shield of faithfulness you bear
    From terror of night or arrows in flight
    Evil stalkers and plagues beware!"
A thousand to ten at my right hand
But never to me shall they come
If God continues my habitat
Punishment only shall I see of the wicked one!
    Disaster and harm will not come near
    For His angels shall guard my way
    Soaring to lift me into their hands
    Kept above the demonic fray.
"Because he loves Me," says the Lord,
"I will rescue him;
Protecting, for he acknowledges my Name
Despite the trouble or how grim.
    I'll deliver him with honor
    Giving long life to satisfy
    Showing him My salvation
    For him on the cross I died."

"A TRAGEDY IN OUR LAND"

We the people, in order to form,
A more perfect Union thought:
That all men were created equal,
Until the unborn question was brought!
    Should our special inalienable rights
    Be presented by "those" who can't fight?
Who'll defend the little ones
Whose deaths are 20 times those done by guns?
    God gave us life, liberty and a quest
    To fulfill our goals of happiness.
Yet we, in our pride, began our demise
By shedding the blood of innocent lives.
    God spared not His own nation of Israel
    When sacrificed children's blood was to spill.
Our land shall be given to those we hate
Because our unrepented sins are great!
The fear of A.I.D.S. and other such plagues
    Are broadcast on the news
    Through liberal, anything goes, reporters
    That scorn the conservatives' views!
Mockeries of Jesus Christ
And child pornography
Are among the list of tactical weapons
Destroying our society.
    Our worship of eye—do$$ar-TREE
    Is passed on by an addiction to: T.V.
Sex, violence, murder, and theft
Are telling our children, "there's nothing left:
    Of morals and integrity"
    Just "Be All that you can Be!"
God gives us grace that we may stand
Above the decadence of our land!
    Help us to be strong and shout our voice
    That such lewdness is NOT our choice!

9

"Congressmen, Senators, hear our plea,
To avoid the judgment of God's decree...
      "That, if My people, who are called by My Name
      Will NOT repent of their evil game,
Their land shall I smite with a terrible plight
And swiftly as, a thief in the night!" "
      To do justly, love mercy, and walk humbly with thy God
      Is all I required of you,
      But injustice and hatred and pride you have sought
      In arrogance to do!
Your banks and businesses
You've credited away
Your once firm economy
No longer shall it stay!
      The humanist ideology
      Into your schools you've preached
      But interest paid on what they've said
      A demon foe's unleashed...
Children with no respect
Thinking they know it all
Situational ethics
Morality shall fall!
      God help us in these last few days
      Before our Savoir comes
      To heed His call and give our all
      So Heaven's eternally our home.

SHS '72

From Kent State on through Watergate
Cambodia and Vietnam,
The Beatles, Hendrix, and flower power,
Uncertainty filled our land.

But fresh from school we embarked,
A chartered course for some,
Invigorated to mold our future
Completing what our parents hadn't done.

College, careers, and misguided ventures
Brought questions we'd never had
'Cause now they are asking us
You know, High School wasn't all that bad.

Why, the kids need help and there's bills to pay
I don't think two jobs are enough.
I need a degree to get a raise
No more is the option of giving up.

It seems my parents kind of depend on me
I feel the drawing of that obligation
From all the years of tears I brought 'em
To a glaring indication...

How math, English and history
Weren't exactly meant to equip me
Yet passing them and other test
Would get me ready to do my best...

Of accomplishing goals that really matter
Not pipe dreams that just wash and splatter
Against the walls of adversity
Blinded by what I couldn't see.

This strength of character and patience brought
Traits that I earlier might have fought.
For respect and authority they often resembled
Yes, they're earned, NOT owed and my pride has been humbled.

A good family and name are cause enough
To put up now with my two boys' stuff.
I raised Cain in school and could have done better
But to raise "My" kids, I'm a dedicated debtor!

"ICE BOX CHRISTIANS"

"What's for dinner? Well, let me see
Seems like some 'good' leftovers."
A drumstick here some macaroni
I'll give the rest to Rover.
    We as covenant people,
    Albeit by god's Grace,
    Don't even give our brother food
    Despite his starved sunken face.
The Bread of Life gave from His table
A measure prepared for the Jews
Yet, drawn by the faith of a Gentile mom
'The Cafeteria' was open for her to choose
    We worry about our spiritual diet
    While others starve to death
    Or if their problems crave toward us
    We glibly say, "There's nothing left."
Are we like Pharisees so callous with our faith
So long as our family's fed and safe, no more can we relate?
    Is our tradition more important
    Than that which God commands...
    To love our brother as ourselves
    Hasn't been the attitude of our land
We're guilty church! Wake up!
We are the moral guide
Whether the court rules God's TEN LAWS
Are left in our outside.
    Little boys need big brothers
    And weekend fathers too
    But our high profile with society
    Leaves a wisp of time for use.
Your business nor your busy-ness
Won't impress God at all

When He's impressed you to help someone
More than a random call.
    As much as you have done it
    Unto the least of these
    My brethren you have done it
    Not to them but Me. Jesus the King!

"THE ROADSIDE REST"

Here I sit at the same roadside rest
Where some thirty years ago
We'd picnic on those concrete slabs
Forfeiting worries and letting time just blow.
    O' serenity of the mountain scenes
    Across the railroad tracks
    Though tall pines have grown blocking my view
    No obstacle can keep memories from drifting back.
That little green Coleman stove
Perked coffee and fried bacon from its grill,
Ah, that aroma from the brisk morning air
How smells make reminiscing so real.
    We all played with our hula-hoops
    Lodging them way up in the trees
    Shot a bear cub with my cap pistol
    While the "brave" locked in the Buick just screamed.
Grandma with her checkered table cloth
Like that would stop the ants
All the milk spilt on my lap
Sure didn't keep them off my pants.
    Grandpa with his stoic stare
    Out over the mountain range
    Shows me now through my own trials
    God's inner peace isn't so strange.
This busy world we live in
With its high-tech communication
Abounds with over-stimulated youth
Who have of their parents NO relation.
    Where is God in this cyber-space?
    Should we take time to listen in?
    Or are the cares of this world too loud
    For any conversation with Him to begin?

Those quaint little prayers from Sunday School
Won't get it in these last days
For God's Spirit says a powerful deception
Will lead many into its haze.
    The Author of Eternity
    Implores you to seek him
    In His Word, prayer, and fellowship
    'Cause earth's outlook is very grim.
Jesus, who suffered sin, death, and hell
Made no light application
That the road to follow Him is free
But upon His personal sanctification.
    I Am the WAY, the Truth, and Life
    To all who enter in
    Accept me as your resource
    Depart from any sin.
The sheep who hear My voice
Quickly I'm coming for
Tell those who've swayed from the faith,
"Return and Open Me, the Door!"

MY UNCLE ROY

NO saddle spurs could dig in
A deeper impression of
The years and tears we've shared with
This man, of whom, we love.
    The greatest cowboy
    I ever knew
    Who kept his "herd"
    And loved them too!
Roy Jackson, how you cared for
Grandpa and M's Ames
Only God could reward such kindness
From your heart which never changed!
The card games and the dominos
    Endless hours played
    Kept Ol'Grandpa happy
    Up till his last few days.
Those witty interjections
You chided grandma with,
Broke up an else-wise boring time
By a merry spirited uplift!
    Oh the fishing trips we took
    Upon even snaky lakes
    Whether the catch was ten or none
    That time shared would elate!
A tribute due one as you
Can't only be given by words
But rather in lives you blessed and molded
Your character was loudly heard
From the saloon gunshot of that window frame
Falling on your head
To a secure Father's figure
Rising above tornado's dead.

I hope I may, at least, try to be
Half the man you were
To give my boys a stature
They also may strive for.
Many great the Lone Star State
Has grown within her lines
But to me 'twill always be
"Roy Jackson" from her vines!

I love you, Roy!

IS "THIS LAMB" YOURS?

The "Passover Lamb" they offered
Yet not to be defiled,
They wouldn't enter the Praetorium
Plotting evil all the while.
 Religious leaders full of the law
 Couldn't see the innocence that Pilate saw.
Yet, fearing a riot and losing his position
Quickly made Pilate change his decision.
 Beaten, scourged, and humiliated
 This "King of the Jews" they berated.
Jesus was offered gall to drink
In order to numb His senses
Instead the cup of God's wrath He drank
Bearing all our offenses!
 He hung on the cross
 By the nails of our sin
 An willingly died
 That we might live again.
Dead in a tomb with no hope it seemed
The disciples resolved to relinquish their dream.
 But Jesus arose and came to those
 Confused and frightened ones
 Confirming His Resurrection
 Giving the Great Commission.
Going through to all the Earth
Make disciples of the nations
Baptize them into "My" new birth
All My commands are your observations
Love your brother as yourself
Cling to "Me" not to wealth $,
Help widows and visit those in prison
Feed the hungry with true compassion

Clothe the naked and give to the poor
Let Heaven be where your reward is stored.
Wait for My coming expectantly
And I shall receive you unto Me!

A 'STELLA' PERFORMANCE

Never a frown did I see expressed
From this precious lady
And ne'er the words "can't" or "no" did she know
To me, it was "yes" or "maybe"
    Oh how this world needs many more
    Grandmas like my Daddy's mother
    Who raised an upstanding family
    Of five girls with one brother.
Her baby blue eyes, which never lied
Cast a happy aurora around you
And those apple pies left no disguise
That a wonderful stomach was warmed too.
    'Twas so many years she stood up for me
    When my parents thought I was crazy
    Saying, "He'll turn out alright, for you trained him"
    Though then, plump and often lazy.
A teacher at heart she'd never depart
From letting a lesson be learned
In practical means her wisdom was seen
A glorious beacon of thought turned.
    Up a hill for blackberries thrill
    She'd snatch them by the dozen
    While cobblers awaited the dough which she kneaded
    And fresh peaches that were frozen!
I loved to run the graceful path
Of roses among her flowers
And yes, this little lady to me
Stands a magnificent tower
    Of hope, confidence and pride
    That in me she helped raise
    So, likewise my generations
    We may honor her and praise

The God she served and returned back to
Her mission done quite well.
May her memories be not just spoken
But lived toward those we tell.

    Heaven's gain was ours too
    For 94 sweet years
    Yet, till we meet her with our Lord Christ
    Grandma's reflection will shine in our tears.

I love you, Grandma Addison.

"CYMBALS OR SYMBOLS OF PRAISE?"

Hallelujah, Hallelujah!
Oh yes, dear LORD, AMEN!
We've not yet reached God's ears, church!
So, let us do it all again.
    Magnify "your" voice not Him
    I want a real crescendo
    Exalt that hymn of praise
    Sing like "my worship" says to.
We all must be in perfect key
Because this song I wrote
Sound the trumpet, blow the alarm
For your missed that last high note.
    Are we gathered in one accord
    To worship us or the LORD?
Holy hands we are lifting
While lust for the world keeps us drifting…
    Further from our Maker's presence
    'Cause He didn't give us all our presents.
Who may ascend to the hill of the LORD
Or stand in His holy place?
He of clean hands and pure heart
Are those who seek His face.
    Is there really power in our worship hour
    With shattered gates of hell
    That wall we wouldn't scale?
Was the cross of Jesus
A losing proposition?
Or salvation for all mankind
A prerequisite condition.
    If we truly love our God
    Then praise for Him exhibit
    For in that type of fellowship
    Our God gladly inhabits.

"ATTITUDES TO BE"

Matthew 5:16

Bless the poor
For the Kingdom's won
Those who mourn
For the Comforter's come
    Bless the meek
    'Cause the earth is theirs
    Those who thirst
    Are filled with Righteousness
Chorus:
Praise Jesus, our Messiah
For the promises He made
Praise Jesus, our Messiah
For His love He freely gave
That our lives He came to save!

Those merciful
Mercy they'll receive
The pure in heart
God shall they see
    Called sons of God
    For peace that you make
    Rewards in heaven
    From taking lies for My sake
Chorus: (Praise Jesus, our Messiah…)

Blessed are you
When they put you down
You are salt
Don't savour the ground
    Let your light
    Shine before all men
    Glorify!
    Your Father in heaven!
Chorus: (Praise Jesus, our Messiah…)

THE PILGRIM'S PROGRESS?

We as pilgrims before us
Have traveled down life's journey.
Yet today, our religious freedoms
Are sought out by an attorney.
    Could William Bradford stand so proud
    to see his colony turn and shroud...
the name of God, "shhh..." IT CAN'T BE MENTIONED.
While the vilest of sin draws all attention!
Would that the Indians we extracted
With their concern and love for Earth
Had kept us from stripping all her resources
and leaving a shameful dearth!
Oh yes, we should be thankful
That God's not sooner judged
The balance of our love for Him
compared to what we've grudged
And clasped to hold on to
Our homes and businesses
Not even considering
These "gifts" aren't ours but His.
The troubling in the air we see
Has been brought on by you and me.
    We've left the faith of our forefathers
    To crave a sensual religion that fodders...
Personal ambitions and greed
"Your feelings don't matter, what's in it for me?"
God help us wake up to our erring ways
And realize how far we have woefully strayed.
May we be thankful for our very breath
Knowing the world's geared only for death.
    But "LIFE" and that more abundantly
    Has God given to those who believe.
A rest and peace amidst the storm
And protection from all spiritual harm.

Jesus is coming for a glorious church
When all hell breaks loose on this poor ol' earth.
Yet, to each He's given a choice to make
Help us Lord to see what's really at stake.

A BABY'S PRENATAL PRAYER

LORD, protect me from my mother
And her government
The attacks levied by "Big Brother"
Seem they'll not relent.
    Please stop their trips to London,
    A tour to terminate…
    "me" from her life because mine
    Didn't fit in hers so great.
Well, R.U. 486?
No, I'm not thank you
For it stops the blood to my veins
A horrible thing to do.
    Starve me, burn me, tear my limbs
    Lord, what did I ever do?…
    Than follow "your" plan of creation
    To fellowship with you.
Mother Teresa said, "abortion's murder,"
To the President and Mr. Gore
While the audiences' response was standing
Our leaders sat staring at the floor.
    LORD, do they not realize
    This innocent blood cries out…
    "Justice will be required,
    And "Your" judgment's coming about."
I pray most for my mother
That you would touch her heart
Now, while the comforters of "her problem" come
With their folly to impart.
    God help the other mothers too
    Languishing a decision
    Let them know that "Life" is right
    And "you'll" be their Provision.

"A DECADE OF TRIALS"

Well, Sun, it's been 10 years now
Since our marriage did consummate
Many troubled waters we waded through
While other times were great.
    I'm surprised you haven't shot me
    For those crazy moves of the past
    I'm more shocked that you held firm
    To make our union last.
I know I don't speak many words
And my feelings are camouflaged
But without your devotion to me, Sun
A huge void in my heart would lodge.
    I deeply appreciate
    How good you've been to the boys
    And when I'm bummed out with my problems
    You try to bring some joy.
How fortunate to have a woman
Who's smart and pretty too
You're thrifty and blatantly honest
My schemes you always see through.
    It's been so one-sided this past year
    With you carrying the burden of work
    I pray some way I can repay
    Your time and aches that hurt.
I wish we still had the essence of youth
Flowing in our veins
Or some way that you could keep proud of me
So your confidence wouldn't drain.
    I love you, Sun, and that may seem shallow
    Compared to what you've gone through
    Just work with me the next 10 years
    And I'll do all I can do.

"A YEAR AFTER"

How long at the grave do we mourn
Grieving over the past?
While eternity's but a breath away
We should rather yearn for that which will last.
 Why seek ye the living
 Here among the dead?
 Did her spirit not rise with Me
 As My Word has clearly said?
Resurrection is but retrieval
Of a body long since perished
One to Heaven, the other to hell
Contingent on whom they cherished:
 The lust of the world and selfishness
 Or love for God and His Righteousness?
 Redemption through your own intellect
 Or purchased by Jesus' blood did you select?
 Accumulation of wealth and fame
 Or acknowledging sin's guilt and shame?
 Faith in man's religions of works
 Or humble adherence to Christ's finished work?
Jesus will soon be returning
For those who long for Him
While foolish hearts that have feigned their love
Will see this Advent as totally grim.
 "Oh determine NOW dear children"
 Would be our mother's plea:
 "You cast off any encumbrances
 That would keep you from coming to me."
Find the Way in God's Truth
For your Life it is Jesus
Hold firm to His love for you
And soon you'll come to see us.

MY SOLILOQUY OF RYAN

My first born son I was so proud
Then responsibility hit
Could I be a decent father to him?
Or was I totally unfit?
    I had not known a father's love
    So what was I to share?
    Would he sense my concern to give him a good life?
    Or would he doubt that I even cared?
It seems all I do is wrong in his eyes
He says he'll run away
Breaking my heart in fear for his safety
I wonder what good I've done to stay…
    And put up with his vicious words
    Such bitterness poisons my soul
    Searing pain from him not listening to me
    Shatters already brittle nerves out of control.
Maybe I've tried too hard
Or maybe not hard enough
It seems that only a loving parent
Could endure this relentless stuff.
    God give me the grace and patience
    To guide this dear child of mine
    Oh may he relish the memories
    Of our effort and our time.
Thank you, God for your mercy
That stayed with me despite my sin
I pray that my prayers, as my mother's for me
Will bring Ryan's heart to you again.

Love,
Dad

"THE CHURCH MORGUE"

Are we monitoring God's heartbeat, Church,
Or are we clinically dead?
The tests reveal His Word to us isn't real
For we have done little if any of what He said.
    If we are called to be His witnesses
    In this court of life
    Then for perjury we should be held
    'Cause our testimony sure ain't right.
"You say you are a Christian?"
"Yes, truly a disciple."
"Then let Me interrogate your lifestyle."
"Objection! Your Honor, that's personal."
    "Objection over-ruled
    For works do testify
    Whether you're living in the Truth
    Or living in a lie."
"Judge, in my heart, I really love God."
"Not if your brother you hate."
"How have I missed it this time?"
"By not telling him of Jesus and that the hour's late."
    "But my job, the traffic and hassles at home
    Leave little time to fit this in."
    "That's irrelevant to the cost of one man's soul
    You must accept that you're strategically positioned."
Love Me and keep My commandments
In everything you do
Sow into the lives of other men
So your works will follow you.
The "Seed" you need not worry about
It's the ground that must be plowed
Speak Me, Praise Me, Serve Me.
The rains for growth, I control that cloud.

If you'll die to self interest
And let Me in your plant
A crop with My potential
The harvest will seem instant.
Many are called yet few have chosen
To answer My High summons
Just as Adam, you have no excuse
Not heeding My voice when I'm in your garden.
    Your life may be required of you
    When iniquity abounds
    Unless you're fitly joined with Me, The Word
    A deep hole for faith will be found.
Exhort the Body daily
And sense My spirit's flow
Keep your mind rigidly alert
Make the talents I've given you grow.
    Quickly, oh so quickly, child,
    You must prepare for war
    Lucifer's legions are mounting
    Set to unleash the evil they've stored.
The assignments I send are crucial
Don't hesitate when you're sure you've heard
For a strong offensive you'll move in
Wielding My Spirit's Sword.

MORNING MERCIES

Petals of love from the flower of your youth
"Bruised" yet now they are blooming.

A radiant glow fills dark voids of our past
Joy displaces an anguished heart

Horizons of hope when it seemed we couldn't cope
Sparkle in our eyes dries tears from sorrowed cries.

Jesus gives this joy, strength, and peace of soul
Rejoice and worship Him and let God work within.

Sweet fragrance flows from my heart to impart
Oh bless the risen Lord for His precious Word!

"BRIDGES TO CROSS"

Rushing streams o'er waterfalls
Gleaming with life within
Relaxes our racing minds which fret
About problems of but a temporal end.
  How often the Eternal we put off
  A destiny we ALL must face
  Just get a little more in this life
  Is the common theme most people embrace?
When time's no more and judgment has come
A wisp of vapor describes all man has done.
  Apart from the high call God has shown for His man
  No rewards will be offered our frail human plans.
The creator of Life, of which, we enjoy
Ask but our hearts and service to employ.
  O' Father God use us
  However you may want
  Let me never be selfish
  Nor quit at any point.
I Love You, Jesus
I can't thank you enough
That you've planned way beyond
All this temporal stuff.
Dear Mike, I pray this poem may say
A little of what I feel for you
Dealing with stress and all its mess
Your once firm bag of patience, has any holes worked through?
  Yes, God's strength is and added dimension
  When our trust and mind's on Him
  For He who began a good work in you
  Will see it through much to devil's chagrin.
Mike, you've been a great witness to me
Through the fiery trials you have fought

Amidst the school, work and stretching energy for a WIFE
Not to mention sweet Heather you lost.
But for 40 you are lookin' good
A prime specimen of health
Now what you train your family to be
Will account to what matters for wealth
For all we leave is our progeny
And you have some very fine ones
Bless them, pray and lead them to God
Then your WORK will be done!

"A FATHER'S PRAYER"

I. Father in Heaven, it is You who are Holy. I pray that Your Kingdom is fulfilled on earth the same way it is in Heaven with perfect order and obedience to You and Your commandments to: 1.Love You Lord God with all our heart, soul, and mind and have no other gods before us. 2. That we shall not make anything an idol to reverence above You, oh God, including our ambitions, job, wife, family, or any self entertainment or lust that would interfere with Your plans and purpose for our lives. 3. We shall not take God's name in vain through reckless condemning speech, curses, or oaths that we don't plan to follow. 4. We shall honor the Sabbath day to keep it holy. At least one day a week we purpose to rest from our work, reflect on Your goodness, and worship You, Almighty God, in assembling ourselves together in one accord to seek your face and petition the Body's prayers before you and to praise our Savior, Jesus, in spirit and in truth. 5. We honor, respect, and bless the father and mother that You gave us. Their needs we shall meet and their godly council we shall heed. 6. We shall not murder—in thought, word or deed. 7. We shall not commit adultery with our eyes, mind, or any other member of our body. 8. We shall not steal materially nor rob the time we owe wife and family. 9. We shall not bear false witness against our neighbor but we will be trustworthy and faithful in all we do. 10. We shall not covet by lusting after our neighbor's house or wife, their position in life, nor anything that is our neighbor's. II. Father, may our needs be met this day according to your riches in Glory by Christ Jesus. We thank You that you've given us all things that pertain to life and godliness. III. Father, I repent of all wrong that I've said, thought, and physically done and I ask Your forgiveness of my sins against You, man, and my body, which is Your temple. Merciful Lord, forgive these sinful debts that I've incurred as I forgive all who have those debts to me. May I love my brother as myself. IV. Almighty God, who would have no temptation overtake me, but will always by Your Grace provide a way out of the temptation through Jesus, the Door. You lead me not into temptation but You deliver me from evil. For it is Your power and glory that shall last forever. Amen! V. Lord of the harvest, send laborers to those closest to the kingdom. Protect them from harm till they receive Your salvation. Present healing, hope, and deliverance to them through Your Word via the air waves, written correspondence, and ministers of flame and fervor that will unashamedly proclaim Jesus before them. Send Your angels to direct their paths to receive Your hope, love and council. Satan, we bind any interference from them being contacted by God's Word. We bind fear, doubt, hate, evil communications, pride, pornography, confusion, and anything that would exalt itself against the knowledge of God. VI. Father, we lift up before You our President and all elected officials and judges of our land and ask that You would influence and speak to them by Your Holy Spirit so they would love mercy, seek justice, and walk humbly before You, oh God. Guide them and us into the paths of righteousness for Your Names sake.

"WITHIN THE GATES"

Oh the numbness left when you've lost your song
No lift left in your step
Well-meaning words are no use to confer
Even Hugs seem awkward and inept.
    Tragedy pays no favorites
    And sympathy has the best of intent
    Yes, our tenure on Earth's full of battles
    With an enemy who'll never relent.
I'm sorry that I never met Jadie
What a treasure to all she must have been
I sense Christ's return is imminent
With her bumping the angels to usher you in!
    "My Grace is sufficient for thee"
    Often seems but shallow words
    Till the moment it's needed and won't be succeeded
    Without God's peace to soothe your fragile nerves
But by his Grace, Joey, you and I know neither one of us would be alive
I'm sure it hurts and I think I'd feel guilty
To have raised hell and still survived
    But that's from the accuser of the brethren
    "not" from a loving Father
    Who writhes with pain as you do?
    At the loss of your precious daughter.
Such an outpouring of love for your family
Scantly measures the love Jadie's now bathed
While basking in the glory of God
Anthems "she wrote" to the Most High raised!

"YOU SAY"

You say that you love Me
But your works prove otherwise
You say that you're humble
Yet proud in your own eyes.
    You say I'm your Savior
    And you need nothing else
    Then I came to deliver
    But you won't let go of self.
Chorus: Who do you say I am
It's more than just words
Who do you say I am
Live for Me today
    You say you've been set free
    From the deepest sin
    Then turn from My precious Grace
    And wallow right back in.
We're information's generation
And words fill the air
The Word made flesh to manifest
And free from sin's despair.
    Chorus: Who do you say I am
    It's more than just words
    Who do you say I am
    Live for Me today
I'll give you My glory
To bask in My love
Walk in My righteousness
Washed in My blood
    Chorus: Who do you say I am
    It's more than just words
    Who do you say I am
    Live for Me today

I made a promise to My Bride
That I'd sweep her away
Writing invitations on the hearts
For others to be saved.
    Chorus: Who do you say I am
    It's more than just words
    Who do you say I am
    Live for Me today

"ECONOMIC WOES"

Dear Sun,
I'm sorry for my anger
I'm sorry for your pain
I'm sorry for the lack of work
Please let me try again.
    All the pride a man should have
    Is that he does provide
    And having you to work or be without
    Hurts me deep inside.
I love you and will do for you
Whatever it may take
But please don't scorn my attempts
For only that can break...
    A heart that's already confused
    Wondering what I did wrong
    Or how I lost your confidence
    In me that made me strong.
I'll do my best for God's dear help
To make it o'er this hump
But hold on with me precious wife
This struggle may more than bump...
    Our style of life or what we think
    We should or shouldn't have
    Just trust God for His provisions
    Then rebound back instead.
The righteous shall not be forsaken
Nor our seed be begging bread
'Cause blessed are those who follow God's
Spirit as they are led.

"X-FILES"

Generation X is not lost
Though they are seeking direction
X is next to Y you know
Yah is their protection.
I see their heart and hunger
Be to Me a powerful witness
Glorify Me, not things,
Fire from Me comes in My presence.
Suffer the children to come unto Me
For of such is the Kingdom
Did I not say in My Holy Word
That a little child shall lead them?
Bless the youth and support them
Your home and all you possess shall prosper
For out of the abundance of you loins
My world shall hear the Gospel.

"DEAR DAD"
LETTER FROM MY DEAR SON

It is late at night and I have been thinking a lot. One thing is that I want to Wish you a Merry Christmas. The big thing is that I have been thinking about how thankful I have a father like you. You have always been there for me and you have always been one of the greatest influences in my life. I cannot explain how grateful I am for someone so passionate and loving as you. You are the most loving father ever and I definitely know you care about me. I appreciate all the things you have helped me with and all the things you have done for me to be successful. I have convinced myself finally that I want to succeed and I am going to succeed…because of you, dad. If I did not have you dad, I would not be anything I am. You have not always lived with me, but I am always thinking of you and how much I want to be like you when I grow up. When I become a father I want to be just like you. I could not ask any more. I look at your picture you gave me and think to myself "everything" I do is for you…All of your hard work will pay off no doubt. I will be the best I can and not give up. Dad, I wish you could be with me everyday because if you were I would have never made so many mistakes. Dad, I cannot express how much I love you and how glad you are my father. No one could ever replace you. You are a big jokester and it is beautiful how hard you try to be happy and good with God. I want to portray myself like you and treat my children one day like you have. I'm sorry I could not give you a gift but here is my LOVE in words and I will always love you and be there for you NO MATTER WHAT.

Thank you, Jordan

"STATE OF EMERGENCY"

Are we in God's will or way?
When tragically we forget to pray
We're sheep of the fold who hear their master
Then approachs the "wolf" and we run faster.
    That same voice from God, which stilled the storm
    Can keep our bodies from any harm.
    This "Lamb" before the slaughter went
    To pay our sins and now we are sent...
As ambassadors proclaiming His kingdom
Winning the lost souls for God to receive them
No greater love was ever shed
Than that as Jesus hung and bled.
    His cross of torture and shame has stood
    The Christian's symbol for two thousand years
    Yet bearing with our brother's burdens it seems
    Unnecessary and seldom endures.
"Am I my brother's keepers?"
Was Cain's response to God
As the church verbally kills each other
With no remorse from what they've said.
    Why should the world seek to follow?
    An army who shoots their wounded
    Though God implicitly stated
    That we are to build up and strengthen.
"Is any sick among you?"
Then call the elders forth.
Not to discuss his sins against us
But realize his value and worth...
    That part of "your body" is hurting
    Instantly you should sense pain
    Dear God, let us relieve and help those in need
    Apart from selfish ambitions and gain.

As the white corpuscles flow to a bruise or cut
And triage is set up for the most critical
Likewise, we must do all to heal Christ's Body
Not questioning or being analytical.

Gen.4:9; Matt 12; Luke 4:18; Gal. 6:2; Col. 2:14,15

"EMPTY VESSEL"

I sleep by a pile of unfolded laundry
My wife on the sofa, I'm alone.
Abstinence has become a tool of torture
But for God's grace, my flesh would be wanton.
    How can I always be wrong
    When surely I felt I did right?
    Why when I try to please God first
    Does my wife get angry and fight?
I've been to the point as Job
Where I just as soon die as live
Except for my children and disciplining them
Does it seem I have anything of worth to give.
    I wish often I had a good friend
    Who would hang out or call me up
    It's not good for a man to be alone
    A promising destiny for me has ended abrupt.
God let the poems I've written for You
And my heart that I have shared
Be given to those wounded souls
Who felt that no one ever cared.
    There is a peace I long for
    Which wells up tears upon the thought
    A sanctuary with my Savior
    Who gave it all so I could be bought.
Oh yes, I do have a Friend
Who prays for me every day
He feels my heart more than I can express
And lifts me out of this dismay.
    What a Friend we have in Jesus
    Who gave His very life
    He's filled my dry emptiness
    And been the warmth from my loveless wife.

God help me!

"CON"TRARY TO WHAT THINGS SEEM TO BE

This is what happened
"Con"trary to what things seem to be!

On a rainy day my gym workout
Seemed a brilliant choice
Yet, before the first weight was pressed
A heavier burden came in place.
    Was I stupid or just naïve
    To get involved in a scam?
    Though now at the lowest ebb of my life
    Ninety four hundred dollars in debt I am.
I climbed up Kennesaw Mountain
With the thoughts of jumping off
Then considering the stress to my sons I'd bring
I let suicide quickly drop.
    Just the day before I prayed,
    "Lord, I'll never lose anymore money!"
    "Make me a good steward because it's Yours.
    This attack sure hasn't been funny!
God's mercy is new every morning
And He'll give the power to get wealth
For greater is He who is in me
To deal with whatever I have been dealt.
    The thief has come to kill, steal and destroy
    But only one of these three has happened.
    The Lord has come to give me life
    And some way this event will be undone.
All things do work together for GOOD
For those called according to His purpose
So, the rest of days to God I'll still praise
His grace is sufficient to bless us.
    Out of the deepest pit I search
    Where God's Light shines most precious

May Your glimmer of Hope help me to cope
I draw on Your strength Lord and how You sustain us.
I'll not be bitter and pay the debt
Knowing God's plan for me is not done yet
In the midst of all things, I give Him glory
And pray this is never someone else's story.

"HIS HEARTBREAK HOTEL"

Well, since my Jesus saved me
He's found a new place to dwell
He lives down in my heart of hearts
And saved me from hell.
    Chorus: My God is so awesome, baby
    My God is so awesome
    My Jesus so loved me that He died
Satan now has no stronghold
The Blood has set me free
I've been redeemed by Jesus Christ
To live eternally.
    Chorus: My God is so awesome, baby
    My God is so awesome
    My Jesus so loved me that He died
He is the only Door
Through the Heartbreak Hotel
Receiving broken down spirits, baby
Willingly to heal.
    Chorus: My God is so awesome, baby
    My God is so awesome
    My Jesus so loved me that He died

"FISHERS OF MEN"

Ocean sea breeze, morning calm
Sea gulls passing by
A search for shells along the shore
Troubled souls cease asking why.
    Shrimp boats drag for their early catch
    A surf fisher is casting his line.
    The poet's pen fluidly writes
    Soaking in such an inspiring time.
People seek an environment to induce
Deep peace and serenity
Yet unless their soul's at rest
Life is shallow—pure vanity.
    There is a "Fisherman" I know
    Who'll give that rest to your soul.
    His net of Love has drawn me in
    Even though I was full of sin.
He "catches" His fish before He cleans them
While many Christians will throw them back.
Thus we bite the very same hook of rejection
The world feels when in this manner we attack!
    By this you shall know My disciples
    If they have LOVE for each other
    So, be a friend but not to their sin
    Use love as bait to win your brother.

Does "your" bait have any bite?

"ETERNAL CROWN"

Can you not see the Light?
Being blocked by the SON glasses you wear?
Your spiritual darkness is lethal
So is apathy showing that you don't care.
    Awake from your sleep and open your eyes
    The Savior Jesus is preparing to come
    Arise from the dead works of your flesh
    And let His appearing be a welcome
The Olympiads run a race
For yet a corruptible crown
Yours is a marathon for life!
To give ME glory and not you renown
    Don't be drunk with the drugs of the world
    But filled with the wine of MY SPIRIT
    Singing with Psalms and spiritual songs
    Thus your praise I'll gladly inhabit.

ARTIST'S PROFILE

I was a firefighter for 17 years and had worked only small disasters compared to the 9-11 tragedy but I did realize that New York's rescue teams were in dire need of prayer and that was what I was doing that morning. Then, like a flash, I believe that God gave me a vision of the last 4 minutes on board of one of the planes that crashed. At the same time, I heard this song. This was a prayer of many Christians on those fatal flights to family and loved ones that: Heaven is in sight and they're all right!

9-11'S WHITE BOX RECORDER

Dear Mom I have no time
To write this song's short line
My end it seems is near
Though strange I feel no fear
    You told me of a place
    In heaven I would go
    For God's redeeming Grace
    Has saved my sinful soul.
The prayers within this plane
Some intense and some insane
A quiet peace I have
Before my Lord I'll stand.
    Please know this mortal shell
    Not in this life shall I tell
    All that you've meant to me
    'Till those Golden Streets you see.
Rejoice my mom and kin
We're about to enter in
With Jesus by my side
I'm not afraid to die.

"UNITED WE STAND"

In horror we watched as our nation
Was brought to a war we never intended.
Now the freedoms we boast from East to West Coast
Are threatened and must be defended.
    A resolve was embedded in America's soul
    To never back down 'till the reins of justice control.
    We the people though many unite
    And pledge our support for this perilous fight.
God give us wisdom, courage and grace,
And by Your Spirit, defeat all enemies we face,
The battle is Yours with Your army enlisted
Let us carry the cross to those who have missed this.
    Oh Repairer of the breach that allowed this attack in
    Receive our prayers, Lord, "Never! Never Again!

God Bless America!

TRIBUTE TO GROVER CANNON

I sit atop Mount Kennesaw reminiscing of a man who was gentle and yet powerful,
molded like unto Jesus, straight from the Potter's Hand.
    Precious in the sight of he Lord was this staunch soldier of the cross.
    Heaven's gain was earth's casualty resulting from Grover's loss.
    To Grover Cannon, man of God, who served his Master well,
    only encouragement and wise advice to me would he ever tell.
From the seat of his Goldwing to the throne of his beloved King,
Grover Cannon's life passed in an instant, but the honor, respect and love for this man,
Countless hours of praise will be spent…
    For the glory is due his Maker, Grover's humility made it glow
    While his walk of faith spoke volumes,
    So much that his quiet voice
    Wouldn't have to show.
The cannons here are tarnished and old;
Most are bent and will never fire.
Mr. "Cannon's" quick wit was always lit
With a deep love for God that inspired.
    A nutritionist in the purest sense,
    Healthy habits kept him fit.
    The devoted love of Alice and their children,
    Only "Heaven" could've ever topped it.
On Golden wings Grover now shall soar
With a "Victor's" welcome at eternity's door.
Beloved family, please, please, don't grieve,
I'm rejoicing beyond my wildest dreams!
    Eye hath not seen nor our mind hath conceived
    What our wonderful Father has made for those who believe.
    Little time, as we know it, here on earth does remain.
    And yes, as prophesied, the world's gone insane.
Let him who is righteous be righteous still
But fervently for the sinner make time to kneel

And plead the blood of Jesus over those wayward souls
and love and mercy of God to surround them, change their hearts and let
them know.

That Jesus' broken body will make the sinner whole,

His chastisement for our peace will get our minds under control.

The stripes He bore have healed us, the death he took redeems us.

The loss of a son I thought I knew,

But there is NO COMPARISON to God's love for you.
Dear Saints, Let's remember this sweet man and realize the hour is late.
But as for Grover Cannon, rest assured
My servant has done well and is doing great!

We love you, Grover, family and friends.

"FOR DAD"

How seldom we've said, "Thank You"
To those who've meant the most
While accomplishment and honors
For "ourselves" we take and boast.
    The influence that our fathers had
    In molding the men we become
    Should be the standard for our character
    And the "drive" to see our dreams come.
Many ballplayers who excel in the game
Had a father as their coach
Despite how inept he might have been
His dad to him was the most.
    I truly do appreciate
    My Dad and all he's done for me,
    His training and instruction
    To be all I can be.
Any pointer you got for my two sons
Would help a lot I'm sure
For the fine tuning you dialed in my life
Has shown me how to endure.

I love you dad!
Your son,
Bill

"BLOOMING GALE"

Gusty winds atop the mount'
Swirling fragrances of Spring air
Huge creaking limbs bowed as it blew
Blossoms filled those which were bare.
    Pollen, as love, flows to germinate
    Spreading effortlessly
    Fluttering butterflies nestle the rest
    Invigorated by the breeze.
Birds chirping to one another
While Red Tail Hawks majestically soar
Spring is such a beautiful time
Of new births, growth and color.
    Runners panting down the trail
    Missing most of the afore mentioned
    I stopped and shared this glorious account
    Because it is my intention:
That I can thank God for His nature
Freely releasing in some way
So the aesthetic qualities I've seen
Will "spring" life in other's day.

This "bud's" for you Liz!

"THE DREAM OF NADINE"

Nadine, my dreams for me it seemed
Had all but flown away
Yet "New Life" is now emerging
A genesis that will stay.
    Your life deals with antiquities
    That have stood the test of time
    And now your heart searches for "lasting love"
    I pray such endearment will be mine.
When do visions for what we hope
Tangibly appear?
When God's witness in our spirits
Makes it very clear.
    Many are called yet few have chosen
    To hear His earnest plea...
    "Don't heed self proclaimed predictions."
    "Rather fulfill our destiny."
My dear, you're such a catalyst
This chemist fills his vials
With love, energy and wittiness
How this woman has been endowed!
    The wings of her wind bring reverie
    Climaxed by heavenly thought
    God bring this angel closer to me
    'Till a rapturous union we are brought!

"FLIGHT OF THE PHOENIX"

She's on the go that Taryn Nicole
Spreading her wings out for Phoenix
And it may be prophetic though she has not left yet
A sign of dreams rising from ashes of past risks.
>   Taryn is so smart and motivated
>   She could sell bikinis in Nome
>   I pray that her destiny finds her
>   In her new Arizona home.
Such a deep thinker all of her life
I wondered if she would ever talk
But when she does, she doesn't mince words
A rich conversation is wrought.
>   If you don't speak to Taryn in English
>   You might try to in Espanola
>   Being bilingual as she is
>   Will really be an asset where she's about to go.
In China the Golden Phoenix means:
Happiness, hope and much profit
Taryn's heart has more worth than this golden bird
And well blessed with intelligence to use it.
>   City Group's gain may seem to us a loss
>   But we all should want Taryn's best
>   Why, if her crazy uncle hitch hikes to California again
>   At least he'll have a place to stop and rest.
To me, Taryn epitomizes diligence
A trait we should learn more about
She spent more years in colleges
Than all the time it took me to just get out.
>   God bless this jewel in her westward jaunt
>   While the warm Zephyrs blow in
>   Welcoming their new Calamity Jane,
>   Who will shoot for the moon and win.

I admire you, Taryn and have enjoyed your spunk
A softball champion who's a fiery competitor
I don't think Phoenix will be a "short stop."
But do show them the gentleness of your demeanor.
  Please keep me abreast of what's happening
  Through email or give me a call
  I pray that the fine husband who's been looking for you
  Will link up and you both be enthralled.
The "Trail of Tears" was of the Cherokee
Who were driven out by the white man
But yours will be a "Trail of Cheers"
Because you are "Driven" by what I see as God's plan.

I love you and I'm so proud of you,
Uncle Bill

"TO GRAHAM CHRISTOPHER BRUCE"

A TRUE GEORGIA "CRACKER"

Who do we see in this little boy
Not known but, from his birth
A part of me, a part of her
Or part of God's green earth?
　　Can the love between two souls physically be held?
　　Then grasp that precious child you bore and see what he'll reveal!
　　The hopes and dreams which have seemed
　　Vanished from our youth
May generate again some way
As Graham grows to choose.
Observing points of two
Blending in to one,
　　Wonders the mind how in time
　　This weave of flesh is spun.
　　May our influence be
　　Proper and well paced
Not asking the world of him, but giving it,
Surroundings to embrace!
The warmth of love with confidence
Whatever be his trials
　　You'll stand assured to help
　　And walk that extra mile.
　　Oh the blessings that we see
　　God's image He has given
That's formed and engrained
By the lives we're livin'.
Dear Laurie & Greg, train you son
The way which he should go.
　　Never demise nor compromise.
　　His Father's love to know!
　　I'm sure you're proud, and so is God,
　　To gain this grand perspective

So nurture, admonish & love this child
As God to His Son reflected!

Your Brother, Joel

BLOSSOM OF THE ORIENT

This China Doll from Singapore
Cheers me up to sing a more.
A sweet fragrance to God she'll please
With the aroma of faith wafting in a breeze
    Such character she shows
    By caring for her Mom
    Displaying what God's love is
    While herself she feels alone.
Though half a day away in time
And clean across the world
She seems to be close to me
Through internet's cyber swirl
    I pray we may keep in touch
    And see what God may do
    For prayer does break all barriers
    So, till we meet it shall be in lieu.

"A LEGACY OF STRENGTH"

Blake, you finally hit one out
This time, from Heaven's park
However, games that are played here,
The end is just the start.
    My, oh my, what a life you lived
    Blazing in your prime
    Now that torch is proudly passed
    In stride and right on time.
A fighter in the best of terms
His Rail Road Grip, you knew was firm.
    He'd hold you tighter than a crosstie wedge
    Surpassed only by any word he pledged.
Strength of character and strength of mind
Constitute what his family could find.
    Steve, Cheryle and Dick have known
    A father of great support'
    Who'd give the shirt off of this back
    And, if needed, he'd do more.
Though seemingly gruff, this gentle man
Deeply loved his kids
And dryer than dirt his humor would spurt
Then muse you by his wit.
    They say you leave it all
    When you bid adieu'
    But respect, love, and gratitude
    Are left by just a few.
Blake Skelton leaves this legacy
For those he did acquaint
And, while at times he seemed far from it
He now leaves us a Saint.
    He waited for his pitch
    And Jesus threw a strike

Now home's a run in Heaven
With "HIM," eternal life!

God Bless You, Blake!

"A CRIMINAL'S PARADISE"

"Officer, officer, lend me a hand."
"To help destroy your pitiful land."
    Don't hurt those dolphins
    With your nets of snare
    But kill those pesky babies
    They are everywhere!
"Justice, yeh' mercy,
Judge, give me a break,
That gal' turned me on
I couldn't help but rape."
    Gambling, drugs,
    They're all part of life
    So, let's legalize them
    And settle the strife.
I sue you, you sue me
We don't have room, set the criminal free
    How did the T.V. settle that case?
    Out dated laws no longer have place.
Those Savings and Loans
Who royalty blew it
Now get out earnings
To go back and do it!
    Freedom of speech
    That we once had
    Is left in the hands of those
    Who tell **us** what's said.
A nation who kills their next generation
Living to gratify these sensations…
    Of sex, greed, power, and lust to control
    A horrendous end shall be their final blow
God's apology is due
To Sodom and Gomorrah

If His judgment's not reeked
Upon our tomorrow.
    As John the Baptist well said
    Many years ago,
    "Repent of your sins
    So God's Kingdom you'll know."
Jesus Christ
Appointment is due
To unravel this mess
But First He wants you.
    It's not a religion
    That will change our world
    But rather a relation
    With God that will swirl;
Mental walks and prison halls
That find the most sorted soul
Down satan's abyss to God's sweet bliss
Of love you will come to know.

God Help us!

"A THANKFUL AMERICA?"

Life, liberty, and the pursuit of happiness
We're endowed by our Creator yet some things we have missed.
    Our liberties were battled for at a terrible cost
    And should they not be defended they will soon be lost.
Is our patriotism only for a safe home and warm bed
Or will we fight and write with those who have fled...
    To keep these freedoms to pray and proclaim,
    "That, if my people who are called by My name
Will humble themselves, repent, and seek my face
From heaven I'll hear, forgive their sin and heal this place."
    We'll not cower to terror nor run from it's fear
    But abandon to our Lord God who ever stands near.
Yes, we are truly thankful for the power He has given us
Not of missiles and military strength
But His Spirit which dwells within us.
    Our Pristine parks we still love and enjoy
    Yet, from our homes we pray as a soldier deployed.
A depth of characters been drawn from America
And a gratitude from what we've been use to.
    God keep our families safe and at rest
    Realizing it's you who has richly blessed.
Your continued Grace we so implore
And thank you for being our risen Lord!
    In the midst of our darkest hour
    How bright His Glory shines through
    Let us look for opportunities to help
    Others receive God's miracles to do.
Yes, we're blessed and most of the world
Is envious of our wealth.
But if we hoard and withhold when we can give
It will eat at us and our health.
    Thank you, Lord for the bounty of food
    And the abundance we all glean

May we never lost sight of your love for us
In Jesus' death so we'd be redeemed.

God Bless America
And our loved ones
This Thanksgiving Day!

"JASON'S PEBBLES"

Along the streams of life
Many may be in the flow
But the nuggets of Truth we glean in the journey
Will determine how much we really know.
    A pretty pebble that's washed over for years
    Was once a jagged rock
    Now beauty has replaced rough edges
    Through pounding pressure and grit.
The Word of Life to those who find it
While some won't even look
But Jason's expounding of the Gospel
Gives a fresh appetite to God's Holy Book.
    If we indeed are Living Stones
    And Letters to be read
    Or precious gems cut by our "Jeweler'
    Should we be hidden, buried and dead?
With the brilliance of the firmament
We're Lights that must shine forth
To a lost and darkened world
Show them God's Glory and the shed Blood's worth.
    Those polished pebbles of Truth we've stored
    Let us rapidly display
    To people who've longed for meaning and purpose
    Convince them that we do know the "Way"
Thank you, Jason, for re-inspiring
What should have never lost its luster
And as a real leader will have devoted followers
I'll do all with God's strength I can muster.

"I LOVE YOU, MOM"

Mom, you always wished you knew
What clicked inside my brain
To make a shield, as cold as steel,
That'd thwart your loving aim...
    At getting through to show you cared,
    Though stubborn barriers brought,
    "Maalox moments," and not a few
    Of endless aching thought...
"Why the bother?" "What's the use?"
"I'm not a real good parent."
Yet all the while, your well trained child
Took more in than what was apparent.
    What you've done through trials has shown
    The character you're made of
    Drawing my deepest respect
    Resolved because your love...
Would not let go nor give in
Despite my past or my sin.
    You always called me, your son, you're proud
    Not to wince or take a shroud...
That would cover any aspirations
You had for me to be
    'Cause your chains of love were to deliver
    A beautiful life that's free...
From warped ideas of how to feel
Compassion or one's worth,
As well as, appreciation
Of nature and God's earth.
    The picnics in the Smokies
    And Texas barbecue
    From Washington D.C.
    Then back to Grant Park Zoo.

All the many years, Dear Mom
Scantly shall ever convey
What you've meant to me in my heart
Until that glorious day...
    When their end will never come
    Because eternity is never done.
    A happy reunion whose Golden Hours,
    Are always cherished because they're ours.
Jesus, Himself has prepared this place
Of monumental love and grace.
Those wonderful qualities I've seen in you
I pray my sons, in me, see too.
    So, Mom, I'll leave you with just this...
    We'll always enjoy God's Heavenly Bliss!

"PRAYER OF PROSPERITY"

Father, You said you would supply all of my need according to Your riches in glory by Christ Jesus and that the righteous would not be forsaken nor my seed......, begging bread and to prove You to the test and see if, as I tithe and give that you would open Heaven and pour out such a blessing that I could not contain it all and that You would rebuke the Devourer, Satan, for my sake so he would no longer steal from me and it is You, Lord God, who causes me to have the power to gain wealth and finance the Gospel and be a blessing to others. You make me the head and not the tail; an overcomer who can do all things through Christ who strengthens me. Because of You, dear Lord, everything I do prospers and has good success and You surround me with favor like a shield and while I please You, You make even my enemies to be at peace with me. Father, You withhold no good thing from me as I walk uprightly before You plus You give me the desires of my heart as I delight myself in serving you, (and the prayers of the righteous are your "delight"). Therefore, Father God, I ask for wisdom, the power to gain wealth, the wealth of the wicked which is laid up for me and I ask that the good work you began in me be completed till the day of Jesus Christ, that my destiny is fulfilled, that I abound with all grace for every good work that You have for me to accomplish in Jesus' powerful name which is above debt, despair, doubt, disease or disillusionment that would hinder Your call on my life. I release Your Holy angels who hearken to Your Word and You said that You watch over Your Word to perform it to go forth and manifest this request. Amen!!!

"JAY'S SONG"

What can one do when you've lost
The winds which blew your sail
Empty, sullen and forlorn
Though once a blistering gale.
    Words seem so inadequate
    To comfort those who grieve
    Yet there is hope that we have in Christ
    Eternal life for those who believe.
I never knew James very well
But I'm sure many others did
Looks like he's got 3 uncles to do some catch'n up with
That reunion shall be most splendid.
    The span of life is only a vapor
    Compared to Eternity
    So make the most of those days you have here
    'Till your dear James, you will once again see.

"A THANKFUL HEART"

The peace of God comes through thankfulness
Though clouds of stress may arise…
Raining pain, fears and confusion
Those clouds "break" when the Son's in our eyes.

Many afflictions come to the righteous
But the Lord delivers us from them all
Being near to our broken and contrite heart
He draws close to hear us call.

These are troubled times which now unwind
Do we stand with God on sure or shaky ground???
Jesus "IS" our firm foundation
With our faith built on Him we will abound!

I'm thankful that he has seen me through
Soooooo many trials in my lifetime
And we all should be grateful for His goodness
Delivered by his Spirit not any power or might of mine.

We've lost loved ones this year and shed our tears
Yet, this life is NOT where it ends
May we relish the memories they've left us
And look to our Lord in Whom we always can depend.

All true things which are noble, just and pure…
Those lovely good reports and things of praise
We magnify You, Harvester of our souls
For Your Grace will keep us through these days.

RYAN'S SONG

Father, please forgive me
For I don't know of what I do
I'm tired of being alone
My desire is to be with You.
    What is right or what is wrong
    My mind can't make the choice
    Please God, I'm hurting
    Just once, can I hear your voice?
I've cried then tried to please everyone
When Your acceptance is what I need
Lord, somehow show my pain to those I love
So they won't think this is insanity.
    Mom and Dad, here my cry
    And please don't try to justify
    The confusion I feel, I just don't know
    But I have decided to let go.
Heaven is only a heartbeat away
And that's where I want to go today.

MICHAEL T.

The Fonz and James Dean biked onto the scene
And my parents though, "What has Debbie done?"
Yet, through all the years, and yes, many tears
They acclaimed him a precious son.
    When Mike signed my annual he wrote…
    "To the dopiest guy I ever knew,"
    Which for me back then was a compliment,
    Considering the stupid things I "often" would do.
The Vietnam War called Mike away
Then Marietta to where he is this day.
    Some "hot" Camaros he couldn't seem to keep
    Without them vanishing into the hands of a thief.
One hot summer we's fishin' in a Texas lake
The only bites gotten were those from a snake.
    So, Mike with a rifle began to take aim
    And blasted those moccasins to their watery grave.
We walked from the lake still talking of snakes
With "brave" Mike holding his gun
Along came a friendly dog from behind Mike's sight
Licked his leg causing "brave" Mike to drop the gun and run.
    A great ball player and joke teller
    Witty humor from Mike makes us glad
    He and Deb brought 2 wonderful girls to this earth
    Kelli and Taryn are so proud of their Dad.
A big brother to me since I was fourteen
Not a better friend could a person have
I'm most grateful to Mike for his help to our Mom
And his comforting words to our Dad.
    A fellow Firefighter and leader of men
    By example and not by rank
    Though he'll retire, Marietta should aspire
    More men like Mike to whom we can thank…

And give honor for his service to all of us
I pray he and Judy have great days ahead.
Just know Mike how the trails you blazed in your life
An awesome impression in me was bred.

INSPIRATION AT THE GATE

One day as I was entering the Kennesaw Armory, a gentleman in a red pickup removed himself from his vehicle and approached me with trepidation. I listened to him as he hesitantly explained that he wanted to wish myself and the men and women of the Armed Forces well. He handed me a wrinkled and photocopied piece of paper that I thought appropriate to share with all of you.

ON ANGEL'S WINGS

Enemy fire, friendly fire
There's shooting everywhere.
I know my mission and will complete it
Though a comrade's betrayal was a scare.
    Freedom and weapons of mass destruction
    Cannot co-exist
    When one is meant to destroy us
    And our freedom so we must resist…
Regimes and madmen like Hussein
Appeasement is not an option
For the last Gulf War has proven that
Doing nothing will reap a greater destruction.
    God bless our troops as they advance
    Comfort those whose loved ones have fallen
    Push the enemy back between "Iraq and a hard place"
    Until Baghdad itself is taken.
Oh give our leaders discernment
To know who are really our allies
For those who would sell weapons to fight us
Only proves that their trust is a lie.
    Lord, may this war quickly end
    And the Iraqi people liberate
    Let us NOT rejoice in military prowess
    But in you, Lord, who alone is great.
Some of the world may look upon us
As the 'Big Bullies from the West'
Yet, I submit if these people were threatened
All too soon the battles they'd contest.
    We've traveled through sand and the grit of war
    Not for oil, or for personal valor.
    Please let us unite till the end of this fight
    And proudly show what America stands for.

Lord, continue to protect our troops abroad
Oh angel's wings you have bore
Bring them safely from all treacherous throes
To a united United States shore.

Note from author: Upon sharing this poem with US Naval Intelligence Officer Jeff Mansfield it was determined that this should be should be displayed for the Armed Forces to see. So, it is proudly being displayed now at the U S Pentagon.
THANK YOU JEFF!

IN MEMORY OF THOMAS TINSLEY

Thomas, Oh Thomas
How does your garden grow?
Hard work and tender care
And just lovin' it is all I know.

Those tactics used seem a lot like
The family which Thomas and Jeanette raised.
For Michael, great and grandchildren alike,
This man should really be praised.

Steady as the day is long,
His humor he'd freely share.
If ever a need or crisis arose,
Thomas Tinsley would always be there.

The Bible says, "We will know all men…
By their fruit, whether good or bad."
The crops sown by Thomas in his life
Were evidence of a successful Dad.

Many a son dreams to have had
A relation like Mike to his father.
How appropriate it seems for him to have died
In his son's arms on the way to God's hereafter.

This man I've always respected
And gleaned from his calmness under fire.
I hope some day that my own two boys will say
As Mike has, "He's the best Dad I could ever desire."

I pray God will comfort Jeanette and all his family
And may I truly express how you have blessed me.

The beauty of Heaven, no one can compare,
But I'm sure Thomas will enhance it up there.

He may have come to the "Garden" alone
But Jesus was there to meet him.
Soaring to his new destination
Where we longingly look to greet him.

"TUPELO HONEY"

Amber came to this earth early
And sadly left the same
Collecting sweet nectar from us
Not for her use but for ours was her aim.
    Such a delicate blossom though bruised
    Inspired us on how she could cope
    While her life was on trial all the while
    Her concern was for teaching and giving others hope.
Amber's beauty was much deeper
Than the pretty face we saw
It was love, joy, peace
And gentleness from God she would draw.
    I don't understand how pain can so brand
    Good people when they are in their prime.
    But, I'm not God and don't claim to be
    For He's not moved by our view of mortal time.
Some live a long, fulfilled life we say
And that a brief one isn't fair
With good and evil living side by side
They still exist and breathe the same air.
    Yet, the impact they had on what they did
    Before God and their fellow man
    Will be recorded in His Book of Life
    Which secures an eternal plan.
Jesus knocked on Amber's heart
And she gladly let Him in
I guess He liked His stay so much
He asked her to stay with him in Heaven.
    We had a party once at Mike's
    When Amber was but four
    As the hours went past her bedtime
    For her rest they closed the door.

This bubbly child kept bouncing up out
To see what's going on
"Honey, we're having a party"
But she needed to know what that was before the dawn.
    After the 3rd time little Amber
    The word "party" she still didn't know
    Replied to us, "If I can just taste it,"
    "Then off to bed I'll go."
Eye has not seen nor ear has not heard
Nor has entered into the heart of man
The things which God's prepared for those who love Him (1 Cor 2:9)
And experiencing this glory our Amber now can!
    A man had asked God, "Where were You?"
    "When my precious son died?"
    And God's reply with a tear in His eye;
    "The same place when My only Son died."
The sweetness of Tupelo Honey
It's pleasant taste lingering in your mouth
May God's presence and love touch each of us
Like Amber did when she came about.

LETTER TO RYAN

To my precious Ryan,

You are my first-born son and very special to me. We may not always be together as you may be called to France, Germany or even Korea for some high tech engineering job that needs graphic designs of your precision, so, please take me with you in your heart! I believe not seeing you and Jordan every day and experiencing your lives has been the hardest thing for me since the divorce. I want to impart God's blessings to you as you approach manhood and to share His principles to live by. First, love, serve and honor God in all you do. Second, respect and do right by your parents. Third, be true to yourself, faithful to God and to your wife. There are 3 things I want you to consider as well: 1. The measure of a man is not in what he has obtained but rather who he is in character before God. 2. Faith without corresponding actions is dead. Don't just say that you go to church or read your Bible but prove it by showing the fruits of: love, joy, peace, gentleness, patience, goodness, faithfulness, self-control and kindness which are grown and maintained by your allowing His Holy Spirit to work in you. Ryan, I have not always operated in even some of these traits at times and I wish I could take back the angry times I had with you. I saw so much of myself in you when that rebellion arose, I wanted to quell it by whatever means it took and I do apologize for that. I want you to pursue and develop your gifting and not to take them as a hobby like I did. God gave those gifts to you and, just as Eric Little, the Olympic runner said, "I feel God's pleasure when I run," so will you whether you are playing a guitar or developing a genius idea for computers. Be cautious who you share those ideas with. Finally, let God bring you a virtuous wife who will always be devoted to Him and you which "IS" being a smart woman that you desire. Psalm 112: Blessed is the man who worships the Lord, who delights greatly in His commandments, v2 His descendants will be mighty on the earth; the generation of the upright will be blessed. v3 Wealth and riches will be in his house, and his righteousness endures forever.

But (Mark 8:36)—For what will it profit a man if he gains the whole world and loses his own soul? Ryan, I pray that will never happen. Instead, if God and His Kingdom and being in right standing with Him is your main focus then all these things shall be added unto you. (Matthew 6:33) Consider, there has been no greater love than that of Jesus laying down His life for us to live eternally with Him by faith in that sacrifice for our sins. When the Bible says to," Train up a child in the way that he should go and he won't depart from it," I believe that a better rendering would be that when you train a child up in a way that he should go that "it" or what you trained him in won't depart from him, even if he sways off the path.

I love you,
Dad

LETTER TO JORDAN

I want to impart God's blessings to you plus some wisdom that has been important for me to learn over time. I don't think you'll ever forget me but please don't lose sight of what I've attempted to exemplify to you. You have a sensitive and tender heart, Jordan, but don't let that be confused with being so self-conscious of your worth as a person that you think you have to be rich to be of importance. You mark my words, "He that is last shall be first and he which is the least in his own self estimation shall be the greatest." This goes for your attitude about wealth and not just wealth itself for it is the "love" of $$ Money not the money that is the root of all evil. That's why the Bible says to lay up for yourself treasure in heaven where neither moth nor rust can corrupt and where thieves cannot steal. A generous and kind heart is to be treasured. He who gives to the poor lends to the Lord and He will repay you. Even though I have been extremely proud of you in baseball and basketball, the most proud I've been was he times when you were friendly and tried to help your blind classmate at Sixes. God takes note of that too. I'm not asking you to take a vow of poverty or anything like that but I do admonish you with 3 John 2 which says, "Beloved, I want you to prosper and be in health even as your soul prospers and that comes by faith and faith comes by hearing the Word of God." (Romans 10:17) Jordan, you have so much going for you. You're smart, very nice looking, an awesome athlete and a lot of fun to be with. I'm just trying to share some things that will really help you later on in life. Learn to be content with what you have and that doesn't mean being complacent or not aspiring to do well and be successful. You need to be happy and not worry about everything during the journey that takes you there. (Mark 8:36) For what will it profit a man if he gains the whole world, and loses his own soul? I pray this never happens to you. Don't be impetuous like I was so many times. That's being angry and impatient because things aren't happening the instant that you think they should or blaming God for holding out on you when you both know that you're not ready to receive it or that a depth of character and appreciation is being rooted in you or some bad seeds of unforgiveness or bitterness is gradually uprooting out of you first. You and I both need to allow God's Holy Spirit the courtesy to operate in our heart to get these things out. Also there are 3 principles and values that I ask you to live by: First—love, serve and honor God in all you do. Second—respect and do right by your parents. Third—be true to yourself, faithful to God and to your wife. These are 3 truths that I want you to remember as well: 1. The measure of a man is not in what he has obtained but rather who he is in character before God. 2. Faith without corresponding actions is dead. Don't just say that you go to church or read your Bible but prove it by showing the fruits of love, joy, peace, gentleness, patience, goodness, faithfulness, self-control and kindness which are grown and maintained by you allowing His Holy Spirit to work in you. Jordan, I'm not perfect but God is and it is He not me who you'll have to ultimately answer to. Jesus said, "If you love Me, you'll keep My commandments," and the sum of those are to love God with your whole spirit, soul and body and to love your neighbor as yourself. If I didn't love you, I wouldn't even take the time to expressly tell you these things but God laid these on my heart to convey certain aspects of life to you and Ryan as you enter puberty and manhood. I pray that you find the wife of your youth and that she loves God and reverences Him and you for without respect from your wife, your lives will miserable. Be responsible and don't be lured to have sex ever until you are properly married to your wife. In the meantime, (1 Corin.10:13) no temptation has overtaken you except such as is common to man; but God is faithful, who will not allow you to be tempted beyond what you are able, but with the temptation will also make the way of escape, that you may be able to bear it.

I Love You,
Dad

WASHINGTON MARCH TO SAVE OUR NATION

In the past, protest demonstrations and marches on Washington, D.C. have been for the government to recognize the cause and for the government to change and accommodate the people.

"Stand in the gap" is for we the people to recognize God as our source NOT government and that we must humbly repent and change. We must plead the mercy of God to give us what we "need" and not the judgment our nation deserves. God will draw near a broken and contrite heart but shuns the proud and arrogant. He wants us to look at where we are...standing in the need of prayer and quit blaming Washington, D.C. for our sins. God holds the heart of our leader in His hand and we must plead the Blood of Jesus over this man, his family and all our congressmen and senators for it matters little as to how many souls across this great land that they will help or harm if they lose their own. We've basked in the Glory and favor of our God for many years but now is a time of reckoning to renounce sin, receive Him and restore the families that built our nation. Pastors return to the Shepherd, not intellect, to guide you so you can lead your flocks. Gird your loins with mercy and truth. Assemble the elders to pray and minister to the needs of your local body of believers "as well as" the lost souls around you. Call on the militia of angels to bring about divine appointments so they can find the Way in the Truth for their life in Jesus who happens to be living with you. Let the Holy Spirit burn through rejection by blessing those who persecute you and say all manner of evil against you falsely for my sake. Those coals of fire are Mine, not yours, to place on whomever you wish. Follow my protocol to feed the hungry, clothe the naked, visit those in prison, minister to the widows and orphans and then I will release My Glory to heal the sick, lame, deaf, dumb, blind and dead thus daily adding to the church such as should be saved. I am an all consuming fire and that's how I want you; all consumed with Me who is everything you will ever need. If you are so caught up with Me, I will catch up with you and we will soar through eternity.

RYAN'S LETTER TO DAD

To my "old man,"

I haven't written to you in a long time, but I s'pose now's a good time. First of all, happy birthday! Anyways, we don't have much time on this earth and I want to say, sorry for all my ignorance & rebellion. I love you and I try to do all I can to help you. Sometimes, my mind is elsewhere & I don't take opportunities to help you when you need it at times, but I wish I did. I always care about you and wonder how you're doing. I'll do anything for my dad, but sometimes life beats me down & I get lost in my confusion & frustration. I live to be a good person and I try to be close with God. I don't go to churches where I don't feel God's presence—I see hypocrites and lies. I can't say anything because I'm human and imperfect and I try to act with compassion and understanding as best I can. Sorry I don't have much money and I'm writing on printer paper with a cheap pen but I want to say some things to my good 'ol dad. We've had a rough life together and gone through many experiences, but I know you're my father and I wouldn't trade you for anyone. Your love has brought me to better paths and enlightened me. Your experience and advice has taught me how to deal with things in my life. I'm strong, smart, artistic and determined and I have you and mom to thank for everything that I am. You'll see my life unfold and the direction I'm headed and though I'm still a bit lost, I have a feeling that I'll have a good life. You have wisdom that dissolves my ignorance. Your creativity has passed down to me and that allows me to express myself and influence others. You have intelligence that has kept me sharp and on the right path. You have the most life and goodness that I have ever seen in a man. To me, you're the strongest man in the world. I'm happy that you're my father. I'll try to make you proud that I'm your son!

Happy Birthday and Love,
Ryan

THE SENSE OF PATIENCE

Do we aim to bless or blame
God when we seem to fail
Speaking all those "promises"
That "guised" to NOT avail!
    The missing "link," which kept our brink
    Receding from the top
    Was lack of perseverance
    That "narrowed" IN our lot!
How often could we have run
The "race" of Life that's set
When just one foot from the Goal
Twelve inches we'd not net.
    Even for the promised prize
    Strict training we endured
    Conceiving our ambition
    Yet, still remained unsure!
Can we truly feed upon
Our Father's Faithfulness
Dwelling in the land He gave
Along with Peace and Rest?
    Is Patience worth the Blessings
    He promised to bestow,
    Or should our "plants" besieged by "ants,"
    Be left NO TIME to grow?
God's not a man that should lie,
Nor one that we should RUSH
Ere our prayers can hit thin AIR
And return back to us!
    You said," If I took refuge
    And put my trust in You,
    Then You'd surround your Favor
    Where NO ONE could break through!

Establishing my goings
Out from the miry clay
Atop the Rock of Jesus
Set free from dire dismay!
    Expectantly we should wait
    With service unto "Him"
    Shedding doubts and frets of debts
    Disposing each of them!
Fear and Faith cannot relate
For God honors but one.
So, take all trials with a smile
And ASK for more wisdom.
    Stir up that gift that's in you
    And never lag in zeal,
    Sincerely constant in Prayer
    To lift up your appeal!
Invigorated by His Power
With Joy spawned of Patience
Victorious we go forth
A Faith and Heart intense!

JESUS IS LORD!

Psalm 37:7; 40:1; 112:1-4; Romans 12:12; 8:24-26; 15:4-6; James 1:1-9; 5:7-11; Luke

8:15; Colossians 1:11; II Tim 3:10-11; Hebrews 6:12; 10:36; II Peter 1:5-8; I Peter 1:13-15;

Revelation 3:19; 3:10.

TAKE HEED, YOU HEAR
WHAT GOD HOLDS DEAR!

Surely I draw quickly night
Those called my "chosen ones."
Pulling them unto myself
Alpha-Omega comes!
    We hear the Spirit and Bride's Voice,
    "For whosoever will."
    Ere "New Jerusalem" is near
    And won't come down until
God shall speak and say, "It's time,
No longer must they wait."
As adorned and quite arrayed
Descend those "Pearly Gates!"
    How God's again to dwell with man
    In "Perfect Communion."
    O, "Look up," ye saints of His
    At the Grand Reunion!
To the thirsty I Myself
Give "water" without price.
From the Fountain of our Lord
Springs forth Eternal Life!
    This goes to the Victorious,
    All these things that I say.
    For I will be to him his God
    And he My Son this day.
But as for the cowards who contempt
With sinners clearly shown,
There'll be Judgment to disperse,
A lake of Fire and Brimstone!
    Bright is the Light of His Glory
    Angelic host He'll bring
    Anthem of Praises ringing,
    Unto our God and King!

In the twinkling of an eye
The "Trumpet's Note" is played,
While the dead rise first in Christ,
Up from their soddened grave!
    Dear Saints, let us never leave
    Our "First Love" at the "door."
    "Outside" our clean white church walls,
    Which NO LOVE can implore.
For Christ's Body must be whole,
Not just a "head" to pet,
'Cause limbless members will latch on
When His love is our net.
    And NOT a rod to shove and prod
    But guided by His Grace.
    And words compassionately spoke,
    Persuasive and well-placed!
We're called to make disciples
Of all men that we've won,
So let's "move on" for Jesus
And get His Work here done!

PRAISE THE LORD!

Mark 4:23-24; 16:15-20; Matthew 9:37; John 13:55; 15:7-14; Rev 1:1-8; 3; 21; 22.

THE PSALMIST

Jill, the thrill that you instill
From your melodious voice,
Makes the hearer's heart lift nearer
To spout a loud "Rejoice!"
 Oh, the notes so delicate
 And crisp as "new spring" air.
 Freshen, warm, and soothe the soul
 In esprit demeanor!
God sees rhyme and harmony
His "heartbeat" to deploy:
Creativeness and His sweet bliss
Surrounding us with Joy.
 That makes our Life energized
 With countenance aglow.
 E'n though the trials may compile,
 We trust "In Whom" we know
Has laid our steps before us,
So we can do our best,
To let His Light in us so shine,
And "be" a Strong Witness!

Psalm 35:28; 51:15; 81:1; 95:1; Colossians 3:16, 23; Hebrews 1:9; James 5:13;

Matthew 5:16; Ephesians 5:19; II Timothy 1:12; Philippians 2:1-4; Isaiah 57:19;

Acts 2:21—22, 33, 38.

PEACEFUL PSALMS

Peaceful Psalms present a "Balm"
Of healing in its use.
Erasing tensions their intention
A calmness to produce.
    Relaxed members each prepared
    Whate'er the task may be.
    Corresponding every joint
    To work in harmony!
The Lord has made our body
Most suitable to work.
In conjunction with each function
To be whole and not hurt.
    Yet, if discord we afford,
    Our limbs and ligaments,
    We can expect to be subject
    To pain sometimes intense!
Since this is NOT the best for us,
God has a "Better" way.
Which keeps us healthy, free from want
When His word's sought each day!
    We're all given different gifts
    To minister His Grace.
    That edifies His Body,
    So peacefully in place!
We should learn how God's concern
To keep our bodies fit,
Is related to His Church,
A Union that's well knit!
    Our bodily exercise
    Profits only little,
    But that's "in time" that we spend,
    "Not" obese acquittal!

A "massage" is no mirage
Of soothing stimulus.
For Vitality is wrought,
Contingent on its rest!

Jeremiah 46:11; 51:8; I Corinthians 6:18; Proverbs 3:5-10; I Corinthians 12:23.

BROKEN GRAPEVINE

May we think o' brethren
Whatever's pure and just.
Letting Christ mount guard our heart
That in Him we put our trust.
    Winsome ways and worthy praise,
    Of Honor and what's lovely.
    Keep the mind in tune to God
    And stop Satan abruptly!
As a man thinks in his heart,
So will his mouth thus speak.
So keep it garrisoned about,
Teachable and meek.
    Practicing the Word you've heard,
    Completely confident,
    Doing all things thru Jesus,
    Who gives to us His Strength!

To Amber Michelle Addison:

AMBER WEIGHS OF GOLD

Your Autumn leaves tail the breeze
Of Rapturous Beauty.
Against the Sky of Bluish Dye,
Exquisitely pretty!
    Lift up your heads and see what God
    Has wrought to please His man.
    Though earth attacked, it's still intact,
    Yearning His Perfect Plan;
Of Days when war will be no more
And Heaven comes on earth,
With Harmony Abundantly
Established from our *birth*.
    Into the Kingdom He has made,
    All Splendor is unfurled!
    Rejoice O Saints at the gate
    Of God's Gracious New World!

THE GRAND FINALE

Whether Heather rather weather
Storms of Life, it seems,
Is turned by a "worthy" via-duct
To "void" its streams!
    Though the show must always go,
    As it was planned before.
    That last ovation's call to stand,
    Will be from "Your" Stage floor.
No helping cast can take the task
Of padding your review.
For the "call" to rise or fall
Depends upon "just you"!
    We see the Second Showing
    In Heaven's Worship Hall.
    With Heather singing, "Glory
    To Jesus," quite enthralled.
There'll not be any tickets,
For this, His Grand Finale.
'Cause passes all are given
His Love thus certifying!

GOD WITH US

Emanuel was born this day
And came to Earth our souls to save.
The Word made flesh though Deity,
He wills that all men be set free.
From fear, death, hate and sin's fate,
To rise with Him on that "Great Date."
When Saints abroad will heed that call
To "Come up hither," not to fall
Again to sin and distrust.
But stand clothed in His Righteousness
Before our God and King that day.
And worship Him ETERNALLY!

BELINDA'S AGENDA

The Beatitudes are Bliss
Of Heavenly repose.
Each one stands virtuous
To whom the hearer knows.
 They're kept by acts of love,
 The Doer's Prime intent.
 Even through the trials in Life,
 Believers won't relent!
Belinda Carter's view is too,
From this same perspective.
That no sin can enter in
A heart whom God's directive!
 Her humble self-*less* spirit
 Is meek, yet satisfied.
 For Heaven's lovely Kingdom
 Is where she will abide.
She'll reap the oil of joy,
While mournful for the lost.
And Garment of "praise" Promised
As she cleaves to her cross.
 The earth she will inherit
 For waiting on the Lord.
 'Cause He rewards the Righteous,
 That "stay" upon His Word!
How Blessed and Fortunate is she,
For Righteousness to Hunger.
Since that appetite is filled,
And left a "drought" no longer.
 God's favor shields her always;
 From mercy she has dealt.
 No menial word can confer
 Her blessing others felt!

Revelations of his Grace
Are "drawn" from her "pure heart."
'Cause God she sees in all men,
With His Love to impart!
    A Peacemaker and child of God,
    Though often persecuted,
    Still she says to sing her Praise
    Of Jesus, Joy imputed!
Dauntless is her walk of Faith,
Despite all lies and bribes.
For the Word and pleasing God
Goes forth to "pace" her stride!
    She is the "salt" to those who're *bland,*
    And Light to the Darkness.
    With Prayers ascending to restore
    The "breach" in great boldness!
She's loving to her enemy,
And prays for those who're wrong.
Testifying that her life
With God "ever" belongs!

YOU ARE A BLESSING!

Matthew 5; 16:24; Isaiah 55:1-2; 61:2-3; Proverbs 25:21-22; Psalm 24:4; 5; 37:11; 5:12.

MERCY
Aiki, Always in Kindness Involved

Blessed are the merciful,
For mercy they have found.
Through ministering God's work,
He makes all Grace abound.
    According to the "Power"
    At work in her spirit.
    She sees the need abundantly,
    Brought to pass and met!
Her merry heart does for good
Those hindered oft' by sin.
Mending their broken spirit,
Healing them from within.
    Mercy asks no questions
    But tenderly responds,
    To avert what's lost and hurt,
    By bearing their burdens!
She completes what's right and meet
Written in God's Law.
Of Love that reigns in us Supreme,
Not looking for a flaw.
    Called to intercede and pray,
    As we would for ourselves.
    Though putting "feet" to our faith,
    Depends upon our "will"!
Nice comments may be well sent,
Yet actions demand trust.
In God's Word whenever heard,
He enjoins "His" service!
    A forgiving heart slow to wrath
    She kindles loving "fire."

Of hot coals that reach the soul.
Where Christ *gleans* their desire.
By proving that His Love's real,
Not just a bunch of "lip."
For this entwines the Spirit's Gifts
To "draw in" and not "drift."

Along the waves of rocky days,
When no one seems to care.
And "catch hold" God's troubled child,
In wringing out despair.
'Cause the Cross has paid that cost
Of hopelessness and sin.
As Jesus was born for us,
No more to enter in!

Mercy sees these every needs
And wants to play a part.
In other's lives to arrive,
With purpose in their heart!
Many will make a motive
To ascertain what's right.
So let us live to love and give,
And keep God's Word our Light!

Matthew 5:7; Romans 12:8, 20-21; Galatians 6:2; II Corinthians 9:7-8; Ephesians 3:20

BRINGING ETERNAL
TREASURES HOME

How long at the "pool" we wait
For a move of God.
Fretting o'er our past failures,
While countless "press" onward!
    If effort's not demanded,
    Results can't be required.
    Though God meets our every "need,"
    He also gives "desire"!
Life or death? God leaves the choice
And wills prosperity,
Yet these be all conditional
Upon what we believe!
    Why God's Word is taught and heard,
    Should evidence in this,
    That "His Glory" is wrought forth,
    Not "ours," lest we should miss.
The hope of a "purposed calling,"
Likewise to subsidize
Our fathomed faith to elate,
And make the "world" realize
    That Jesus lives "big" in us,
    So they're impelled to see
    How Love, Joy and Peace never cease
    Within God's Family!
God teaches us to profit
And leads us in the Way.
But conversation's broken
When randomly we pray.

May our motivation be
His Kingdom "First" we quest.
Pursuing all men's souls for Him
In Love to do our best!

Isaiah 48:17; Deuteronomy 28:1-13; 29:9; 30:6-20; Joshua 1:8; Psalm 37:4; III John 2;

Luke 12:31; 17:14; I Corinthians 4:20; John 4:24; 5:2-9, 19; 5:30, 37-40; 9:7; 15:7, 8-17;

Matthew 3:8; 5:16; 28:18; Mark 4:19-24; James 4:1-3; II Timothy 2:15; Romans 12:2.

REMEMBER WHEN?

I think back wonderin' how things used to be
I think back wonderin' what they meant to me.
I think back wonderin' what it was I saw,
The life I grew to *know* with Grandpa and Grandma.
I think back wonderin' the love they shared with me.
   What I learned as a child, I'll cherish year on end.
   Each heartfelt lesson learned no mind can comprehend.
   For they'll never depart, engraved upon my heart,
   The life I grew to *know* with my dad and my mom.
   I think back wonderin' the love they shared with me.
The times when told, "To work," my duties I would shirk.
Pick cotton from the ground? I's nowhere to be found.
With switch and lemonade, only one came to my aid.
The life I grew to *love* with Grandpa and grandma.
I think back wonderin' the love they shared with me.
   When troubled in my soul, I felt an outstretched hand.
   Then *Love* was energized no more to reprimand.
   The hurt a little boy was felt and filled with joy.
   The life I grew to *love* with my dad and my mom.
   I think back wonderin' the love they shared with me.
Now Grandpa and Grandma are gone to be with God.
I think back thankin' Him for all the things I saw.
Cobbler and dominoes is not all that I know.
For their life lived in me to let a young boy see,
How *love* would conquer all should every effort fail.
   No more must I look back for coming there will be,
   All that which once was loved in one Big Family.
   A mansion in the sky whose maker is our God.
   I thank Him for His Son, Jesus, my Lord, Who died.
   I dwell in ecstasy from *His Love* shared with me.

BOLDLY TO THE THRONE!

Dancin' in the temple of our God,
Praisin' with our hands and heart lifted up.
Lookin' to the One Who set me free,
Author of my faith eternally!
    Chorus: Well, I worship Him, Jesus! Jesus!
    Well, I worship Him, Jesus! Jesus!
He's comin' for His own and I'll be there,
Rejoicin' with the saints up in the air.
He said, "Be ye Faithful for I m True,
Don't worry 'bout tomorrow 'cause I love you."
    Chorus: Well, I worship Him, Jesus! Jesus!
    Well, I worship Him, Jesus! Jesus!
You cannot contain what's written in your Soul,
So, tell the whole world and make 'em want to know.
His life is alive and livin' big in you,
To heal the sick and castin' our demons too.
    Chorus: Well, I worship Him, Jesus! Jesus!
    Well, I worship Him, Jesus! Jesus!
Savior of the world and my sweet Lord,
God's express image in His given Word.
Sickness and sin He triumphed over them,
Then the devil's keys of hell He took from him.
    Chorus: Well, I worship Him, Jesus! Jesus!
    Well, I worship Him, Jesus! Jesus!
If you can't get excited 'bout the words I've said,
Better check your heart and see if you are dead.
The nature of God is not a "dead entity."
So gird your spirits up and let them PRAISE and SING.
    Chorus: Well, I worship Him, Jesus! Jesus!
    Well, I worship Him, Jesus! Jesus!

Hebrews 4:16

THE BEAUTY OF HOLINESS

The relationship to "Beauty,"
Apart from worldly care;
Is stemmed in God's creation,
Whereby He means to share!
    Like lilies we are arrayed,
    When His Kingdom we seek;
    And let our hearts blossom to Him,
    Most teachable and meek.
Should beauty be just "skin deep,"
Why then aren't flowers ugly?
'Cause the "life" in them is revealed,
Not covered or "flakey"!
    The vibrancy of tulip red,
    Or purple hyacinth glow;
    Brings strong comparison to link,
    How "bright" our Light must show.
Beauty's *read* in folds of Love,
Entwining integrity;
Basking in God's Saving Grace,
Through Christ Who set us free.
    Soaring the "storms" that try to form,
    As eagles rise intense;
    Dwelling in the "secret place,"
    Of God's hovering Defense!
Garments of Praise begin the day,
Adorned in holiness;
While essence of the morning dew,
Awaits us to caress.
    Ascribing to our Lord,
    The Glory due His Name;
    We bow with field and hills,
    Proclaiming that He reigns.

This is the true refreshing,
O' snow-capped mountain streams;
That our Father's given us,
In spirit we can sing!
    From the earth came man's birth,
    With "life" instilled by God;
    And grateful toils have tilled the soil,
    To bear fruit from that sod.
Inherent is the process,
Which nature germinates;
So man prolifically to God,
His Love should emanate.
    Awake! Ye doleful dandelions,
    And realize "Faith" is "Now"!
    No more to slight your plight in life,
    By unconcerning "Brow."
God's goodness and His Mercy's
Been recognized for years;
Yet you hold onto pomp and pride,
Revered by all your peers!
    Let not those "petals" once you held,
    Be scattered from "His course";
    But *grasp* "New Life" in Jesus,
    The All-Sustaining Source!

1 Chronicles 16:29-34; 29:11-13; Matthew 6:29-31; Isaiah 28:11-12; Psalm 25:8-10;

48:2; 96:6-9, 99.5, 110:3; 104:1 5; 1 Peter 1:22-25.

SPILLIN' OR SPREADIN' THE GOSPEL

Spilling comes from a mistake,
When prudence isn't taken;
Like the Word if we're ashamed,
Or care less how it's given!
    The Gospel tune is hewn, not strewn,
    In "trimmed" souls with precision;
    Responsive of His love and Grace,
    Heeding their *decision.*
Prophecy's impending doom,
Is NOT spreading "Good News";
Nor oppressive thoughts which bear,
Things we must refuse!
    Preceding gossip's adage,
    "I'm dying to tell you";
    Should rather stand a prefix,
    Announcing: you're not true!
Oh, give up that lower life,
And scale a "Higher Plane";
Shedding to dust those sensual lusts,
Envisaged with God's aim.
    If we're bent on boxing ears,
    Ours then should be first;
    For the Word discerned when heard,
    Shall not be just *rehearsed*!
Jesus Christ, Him crucified,
And risen from the dead;
Is the *text* not "index,"
Of what God's spirit said.
    "To go into all the world,
    And preach to every creature,
    That Grace and Hope's been manifest,
    No more a 'Coming Feature'!"

God's Zoe Life abides in us,
And we've nothing to share?
With people starved for love and help,
Why don't we seem to care?
 Our Gospel is a package,
 That's gently wrapped in love,
 Containing eternal Gifts,
 All purchased by His Blood!
Does the worth of our "new birth,"
Really come across?
When on "A $SALE$" we missed hell,
Is conveyed to the "lost."
 Are the sick in mind and flesh,
 Drawn to see our light?
 Or do the perishing bewail,
 "I wish those church doors might,
Be brought a little closer,
So, maybe we could see,
If there's Hope *available*,
Wherein we can be free?"
 From lewd desires and hateful fires,
 That war within our soul;
 And give such "peace" to never cease,
 Your spirit will control.
The Gospel is this Power,
Of God to set men free;
From fear, death, hate AND sin's fate,
And live eternally!
 O' faithful generation
 Deliverance is NOW;
 Dorning helmet, shield and sword,
 And really learning how.
The gates of hell are bombed and shelled,
As Praise did Jericho;

So, too, the Gospel we LIVE,
Will let the captives go!

Matthew 4:23; 5:16; Mark 8:35; Ezekiel 11:19; Proverbs 16:2, 6; 15:30; 26:20-26;

1 Corinthians 9:16-23, 27; 2:9-12; Colossians 1:5-6; John 12:46-48; Hebrews 1:3-4;

2:3-4; Ephesians 4:18-25; 5:9-11; 6:10-19.

WINGS OF THE WIND

Windy is the melody,
God's spirit gently sings.
O'er ageless words conceived and birthed
In "fruit" that our mouth brings!
 The Author of the Universe,
 Awaits His Word to Act;
 Seeking to show Himself strong,
 Dethroning all our lack!
Transient clouds form chariots,
And minister a "Fire";
Tempered by the Holy Ghost,
E'en rushing Winds of Power!
 By our words we're justified,
 And by our words condemned;
 But by "His Words" we're satisfied,
 And made complete in Him!
God's given us the Power,
Right and Authority
To carry on Christ's work on earth,
Of setting all men Free.
 No consolations offered,
 For those who only tried;
 Making mental ascension,
 Toward Jesus Christ Who died!
This Man of Galilee, as we,
Is the Word of God;
In "Living Panorama,"
By the things we've *done*.
 Through God's Love, Heaven above
 Will condescend to men,
 Of low estate and the great,
 Where Jesus enters in.

The time is coming, oh, so near,
When that "wind" shall scatter;
For just the wheat to be reaped,
And "chaff" left dispersed matter!
   The "Wing of Wind" bring reverie,
   As those who've made the choice,
   Celebrate high crescendos,
   Uplifted hands rejoice!
Even so, come quickly Lord,
Is our departing song;
Though occupying till He comes,
Will "not" be very long!

Psalm 104:1-4; Hebrews 1:7; Matthew 3:12; 13:25-30; Luke 9:1-6; Psalm 103:1-5;

63:1-7; Colossians 2:6-10; II Timothy 3:15-17; Titus 2:11-15.

IT'S THE ANOINTING

God's anointing is a gear,
Engaged beyond our functions;
Of *normalcy* to "His Degree,"
That draws the Spirit's unction.
    Not by power nor by might,
    But by the Spirit in you;
    Keeps the oil of gladness lit,
    While "inner strength" continues!
Rendered sure God's Promises,
Established in our hearts;
Of Holy Ghost deposits,
Withdrawn when "He" imparts.
    His glorious Word's "Piercing Light,"
    That penetrates the Soul;
    While healing hovers in defense,
    To rescue joints and marrow!
Our Sun and Shield beams His delight,
As we, His servants, prosper;
Bestowed with ever-present Grace,
A "giving life" of splendor.
    Sanctified and called of God,
    We're Love Ambassadors;
    With highest of credentials,
    And "Name" through Faith which conquers!
Is any sick among you?
Then let the elders know;
Wherein you being healed,
God's Glory it will show.
    His anointing stands aloof,
    From pride and arrogance.
    'Cause charity meets others needs,
    For their deliverance!

Invigorated and refreshed,
This oil does symbolize;
Like runners prep before the "Race,"
On course to win the prize.
　　And *Goal* that's set before us,
　　Should never we disdain;
　　To preach and teach the Gospel,
　　And heal the sick or lame!

Isaiah 10:27; Psalm 45:7; 23:5-6; 84:11; Hebrews 1:8-9; 4:12-13; Numbers 11:17, 25;

1 Corinthians 1:21; 2:4; II Corinthians 1:20-22; 1 John 2:20, 27-28; Zechariah 4:6;

Exodus 31:3; II Chronicles 20:14.

TO SONSET MINISTRIES FOR YOUNG MEN

To Whom the "Sonset" Free!

Our lives before we knew the Lord,
Are past and gone away;
As revolving of our earth,
A "Sonset" will portray.
 Yet still we keep on livin',
 Though from a different realm;
 To have His Blood forgiven,
 And Jesus at the helm.
Atop our soul and spirit,
God's word to guide us right;
And "be" a Sword in battle,
His Spirit is our Might!
 No more to be condemned,
 For *missing* it somewhere;
 But having fellowship,
 Of Saints to love and share!
As far as east is from west,
Our sins have been erased;
'Cause whom the "Son set" free indeed,
No "Bounty" can be placed!
 A useful hand is taught,
 To exercise his palm;
 And kind words to the "lost,"
 Present a "healing balm"!
Young men, you are God's Image,
Whate'er the world may say;
May a grip upon their lips,
Be for *those* whom we pray!
 An army God is raising,
 Of "fine men" just like you;

To win the world for Jesus,
And leaving not one clue.
That to them you're a witness,
Of His effectiveness;
In changing lives for better,
Relieving all duress!
I pray all your endeavors,
Be Blessed and have God's speed;
And share Christ's Love to others,
So they, too, can receive.
The Hope of Glory in you,
And that same Peace of Mind;
Seeing our God's Saving Grace,
No more to be left blind!

I salute and love you,
Joel

BROTHER OF THE SON

What to give the man who has
Everything he could need;
But to offer "gratitude,"
For God's love which he breeds!
    Solomon, with all his wealth,
    Lacked prosperity;
    In applying *head* wisdom,
    Around sensual decrees.
Though he got back on the track,
Hard lessons had been learned;
Like his father, David, said,
"The truth must be discerned"!
    Oh, the man whose Love's in check,
    Keeps his life "well balanced";
    Blameless toward his loving Lord,
    Exerting all his talents!
Pure and loyal this man stands,
Sanctioned as a servant;
With countenance of our "King;"
Whose Wisdom circumvents!
    His Words are like a well spring,
    E'en flowing free from slime;
    Of rakish accusations,
    That sway and corrupt minds.
The path he's chosen to follow,
Is guided by God's Light;
O'er troops and walls through temporal halls,
Ascending "up" new heights.
    From glory unto glory,
    Dependent on his "Trust";
    That diligence of our Faith's,
    Rewarded to the Just!

The memories the present brings,
When shared by one who cares;
Releasing thoughts of joy and peace,
For those with souls impaired.
    Stout in stature and in heart,
    No compromise he'll take;
    Adherent of Integrity,
    Reproving *all* that's "fake"!
The face of Jesus has been shown,
In this sweet man of Grace;
So, giving him love and heed,
Is proper and suffice!

II Samuel 22:20-36; Psalm 18-20, 25-29; 15:1-5; 16:11; 21:1-7; Proverbs 3:1-10; 4:23;

Romans 12:16; II Peter 1:5-8; Hebrews 11:6; 12:11; Acts 8:6; II Corinthians 4:5-7;

15-16.

THE REWARD

Talents used as power fused,
Respond when they're discharged;
But the "fuse" which you choose,
Can stay small or *enlarged*!
    Our life is like a catapult,
    We crank it short or long;
    Ere the Kingdom of Heaven,
    Is taken by the strong!
Teresa Edward's "launch" has been,
A valiant one to share;
So relate her life's estate,
Wherein you may compare!
    A humorous disposition,
    Draws quick her state of mind;
    Established by a merry heart,
    So teachable and kind!
She's cultivated knowledge,
Well able to absorb;
More to feed her students,
Beyond the "Spoken Word"!
    Not a sham, but the Truth,
    Spreads this Life of Purpose;
    Excited by the Holy Ghost,
    Fulfilling what God gave us.
Soft spoken and easy goin',
Denotes a quiet assurance;
Of prayers shown from the Throne,
Amid her bold compliance!
    Adorned with robes of Righteousness,
    E'en who she is in Christ;
    Making her countenance "AGLOW,"
    Illumined by His Light!

Her gentle smile could take a mile,
And stretch it to the moon;
Then array that longest day,
To extend more than June.
  Diligence is the "Reward,"
  For those who won't relent;
  From the Word which we've heard,
  Held firm with God's intent!
O' the warm sensation felt,
When God's Love in us flows;
As "passion" gushes through the heart,
O'erwhelming head to toes.
  Her race is never shortened,
  Until she wins the *prize*;
  Of reaching God's perfection,
  To see MAN through "His" eyes!
Enraptured by her "beauty,"
That's pure and not cosmetic;
Like the dawn of a spring morn',
In taste, quite aesthetic!
  Disciplined is her "temple" kept,
  Holy and well shaped;
  Decored by humility,
  O'er faithful windows draped.
Quick forgiving and slow of wrath,
How special is this maid;
Who blesses all she contacts,
In "earnest" as God gave!

Proverbs 14:27-33; 15:13-15; 17:22; 31; Matthew 5:8, 12, 16; 11:12; Hebrews 13:5-6,

9, 15; 10:35-36; 11:6; 1 Peter 3:4; Psalm 96:8-9; 1 Corinthians 3:8; Isaiah 61:10;

Ephesians 3:20-21.

THE AIR OF PRAYER

No strife should dwell among us,
The brotherhood of Christ;
So pray that "it" be resolved,
And "cease" at any price!
    Ne'er the prophet or his wife,
    Should you rise against;
    But pray there's peace between you,
    Where God's wrath may relent.
Just fear of plagues cannot save,
In prayers of selfish mode;
Yet those that yearn from hearts who've turned,
Are "received" in God's code.
    Although we've obtained favor,
    We still need KNOW our Lord;
    Perceiving all He's taught us,
    Observing to do His Word!
There's many prayers we lift up,
But one must by the *first*;
And that's for Christ to come in,
To give us our new birth!
    A man without a kingdom,
    We were before we were saved;
    Yet *NOW*, by faith, prayer and love,
    We reign until the grave.
Oh, Lord! The strength that Samson,
'Twas given to destroy;
Be graft in me to meet man's need,
As Your love I employ!
    Our prayers are like a telephone,
    Should we not dial direct;
    O'er aimless flaws that, "God *must* call,"
    When our *line's* left in neglect!

Turning from our wicked ways,
With "humble posture" pray;
In earnest supplication,
Where God "hears" what we say!
    The destitute He'll not refute,
    But gladly show His mercy;
    While rendered hearts to God impart,
    Reverence of his Majesty!
Gentle hands of our Dear Lord,
Were laid upon the children;
When before He'd pray His men would say,
"Why waste Your time on them?"
    But such is the Kingdom of God,
    And like manner we enter;
    A little child in Jesus,
    Where there is ne'er a "detour."
Have we robbed God in our prayers,
As Jews in Malachi?
With selfish request, "We be blessed,"
While hungry souls should die?
    We're told to pray for others,
    So that we may be healed;
    From motives which are deadly,
    O' pride you've GOT to kneel!
Our spirit is a channel,
We can't afford to clog;
With strife and accusations,
That return back to flog!
    How can there be agreement,
    Except we walk with God;
    And *constant* harmony we need,
    To speak the Truth in *Love*!
One accord heart, soul and flesh,
And called to enter His rest;

Free from want, despair or care,
Devout to God in all we share.
　　Timely works and giving tithes,
　　Should be handled by Grace;
　　Through our prayers to see no error,
　　Will hinder where they're placed.
Consecrate your lives to God,
And He'll enrich those hearts;
Fixed on Him, held firm in Love,
'Cause He'll never depart!

Genesis 13:8; 20:7; Exodus 10:17; 33:13; Judges 16:28; II Chronicles 7:14-15; Psalm

66:18; 102:17; Matthew 6:12; 9:38; 19:13-15; 21:13; 26:41; Mark 11:22-26; Luke 18:1;

22:32; John 15:7-8; Acts 4:30-33; 6:4; 10:4; Romans 8:26; 12:12; 1 Thessalonians

5:17-24; II Thessalonians 1:11; 2:1; Hebrews 13:18; Philippians 1:9-11; 4:5-9;

Ephesians 6:18; I Timothy 2:1-8; James 5:14-16; 1 John 5:14-16.

MAGGIE

Glistening off the crystal brook,
Reflections draw the young fawn's look;
Upon the memories gone past,
Which makes her gentle heart beat fast.
    Those chestnut eyes begin to roll,
    O'er future dreams to unfold.
    Then, all at once, she leaps the stream,
    Knowing now of what she's seen!
Her aesthetic beauty's pure to form,
An image of what God has borne.
When Spirit breathed and earth conceived,
His dear woman that man received.

UNWRAPPED

Gail, the veil of gifts revealed,
Is "drawn" by those who quest;
To minister their talents,
Where others may be blest!
    It is received as heart conceived,
    Reposed though full of life;
    Like words confer their meaning,
    In brilliancy of light.
Tenacious thoughts are often wrought,
While creative dreams flow in;
A warm sensation o'er our soul,
As western zephyr's wind.
    But "note" Who wrote "our" authorship,
    Comes every perfect gift;
    Wherein "His Call" is not to fall,
    Your brother but uplift!
Many things Jesus refrained,
From mentioning man missed;
Yet the one who hid his gift,
Abruptly He addressed!
    Stir up that which is in you,
    And let the world all know;
    Our Father God gave it to you,
    So His Glory may show.
How Wisdom's known of her own,
And His Grace does reflect;
God's Love in us to reach the lost,
Their "need" we'll not neglect!
    What our motivations are,
    Impels us to go on;
    Then with the Joy of our Lord,
    We become more than strong!

The thirsty want His Life which wells,
Up in us as a "Spring";
So give the Living Water, Christ,
Eternally to drink!

Nehemiah 8:10; Colossians 3:16; Matthew 25:14-29; John 4:14, 24; II Corinthians

5:18-21; Philippians 2:1-4; 13-16; Romans 14:17-19; 15:1-3; Ephesians 4:1-8; 5:18-21.

ZACCHAEUS

You seek to see who Jesus is,
But seem to come up short;
So up that sycamore you climb,
To know of His rapport.
    That this man heals and speaks of God,
    As though *He* was His Father;
    Then out the limb of faith you go,
    Where "vision" won't be bothered.
At once, He calls, "Zacchaeus"!
"Hurry to Me, come down!"
While the limb you're braced upon,
Cracks sharply to the ground.
    That which "broke" twas no joke,
    But false security;
    So lodge the "Branch Eternal,"
    This man from Galilee!
Your past is cast before you,
Wherein you chose the "Truth";
Then from the heart you impart,
Those $treasures$ which show *proof.*
    Restoration has been made,
    This little man now stands;
    In stature with the "King of Kings,"
    A "Height" to reign o'er lands.
God's kingdom we must enter,
Before we seek to rule;
'Cause a crown of Righteousness,
Awaits His "Precious Jewels,"
    As clay upon its molding,
    The "*Potter*" will inspect;
    And secure it's "malleable,"
    Removing every speck.

Of fear, lust, and contention,
Which hardens hearts to *stone*;
Till God's allowed that wheel to turn,
And Christ's becomes their own!

Psalm 85:13; 54:14; 1 Corinthians 1:30; II Timothy 4:8; Luke 19:1-10.

BRINGING IN THE SHEAVES

For to live is Christ, but die is gain,
So why then does our life seem vain?
Goals are set and some compromised,
Yet, when they're met, they hold no prize.
    Striving, surging o'er peaks to top,
    While ascended, look what you've got!
    O Vanity of vanities,
    Your prude demure gust thick debris.
In *air* to share with mankind,
Please see the Truth and *don't* stay blind!
A starving world lies at your hands,
Don't let that Salt in you grow bland.
    Why! Knowledge will but puff the proud,"
    This wise disguise became your shroud!
    The "fence" is broken and God's flood's here,
    As His Spirit draws close and dear.
To the ones with open face,
Say, "Send me Lord, I'll run the race!"
For the "prize" is His high calling,
Not the fact that we keep *running*.
    Wisdom learned we shouldn't spurn,
    But hold it lined in God's Word stern!
    Our hands should toil expectantly,
    Knowing God supplies our need!
All is beautiful, in its time,
And success is quite sublime.
If that "inner void" is filled,
By "Christ" Whom our Father was thrilled.
    In having His man redeemed to Him,
    And placed His Crown a priceless *gem*.
    Delivered from Satan's domain,
    And transferred to be with the King!

Oh, dear children, realize this,
Our Father shares Heavenly bliss!
He plants eternity in hearts,
With sense of purpose to impart.
    Then tells us, "Go and reap the ground,
    And seek the lost till they be found!"
    Harvest time's not our *fat field,*
    But the sinners sought and healed!
The tears were sown for his own,
So let us reap those *souls* He's grown!

Psalm 126:5-6; Ecclesiastes 1:11; 2:11; 24-26; 3:1-11; Colossians 1:10-22; Philippians 4:8-9, 13, 19.

MY JOY SONG

Tina, the dream a person could think of,
When cast upon your gaze;
Would lead a believer in miracles seem ta'
Have found one as he prays.
    Lord, I know Your love comes from above,
    And shows through those we meet.
    Sharing the Grace and Knowledge You've given,
    Of Jesus Whom we seek!
Countenance glows when this Saint who has been in
The Presence of the Lord,
Giving Him glory, honor, adoring
His majesty; applaud!
    This beautiful one has shown her heart pure as
    Fine gold or wool of *Lamb*;
    Kept by His mercy, knowing that she's free,
    To serve the Great I Am.
God which is your Shield, Banner, and Faith Field,
That *grows* those seeds you've sown;
Providing for you food, making mountains move,
So heart's desire you own!
    Keep yourself pretty and think of this medley,
    A Psalm I sing to you.
    Realizing my heart I always will impart,
    In everything you do!

Zephaniah 3:17—The Lord they God in the midst of thee is mighty; He will save,

He will rejoice over thee with joy; He will rest in satisfaction that you have no past sins.

He will exult with joy over thee in singing (Amplified and KJV).

THE GARDENER

Where have, my friend, you taken Him,
The Savior of the world?
Left on a cross or in the tomb;
From whence does this Love hurl?
    O' gardener! Is He hidden?
    Or does that Light shine through,
    While even as we talked with Him,
    Our hearts yearned what He knew.
Of Resurrection Power,
Which raised Christ from the dead.
As we, too, must enter in,
Through being "born again"!
    Bearing "fruit" that will remain,
    Must be drawn from Di-Vine.
    With the Word to nourish it,
    Kept *fresh* and quite sublime!
By the "tree" rooted in Love,
A constant crop is wrought.
To feed those "Hungry Souls" in need,
A "Food" that can't be bought.
    Jesus is the "Branch," of which
    The Gardener family stems.
    Sporing seeds of Love and Hope,
    To grow closer to Him.
And germinate all those they take,
E'er yielding from God's Seed.
A hundred fold Harvest of Gold,
That'll store eternally!

John 15:1-12, 16; 20:16; 17:17, 22; Luke 24:32; Romans 5:1-5; 6:4.

ARRAY OF HOPE

Sweet the fragrance fills the air,
As this Dear Saint lifts up her prayer.
To Heavenward with vision seen,
Of Harvest white ready to "Glean"!
   Compassion's known and always felt,
   When through "her hands" she brings His Help!
   Staunch in stature and dignified,
   Her tempered heart's devoid of pride.
No greater love can typify,
This soul who vows, "For you, I'll die!"
Gentle waves create a glaze,
Of sparkle in her eyes.
   Adorned with humble praises,
   Her "well spring" ne'er runs dry!
   Virtuous and beautiful,
   God adds to her His strength.
To be a vibrant witness,
And show His love's the "link."
Consistent, caring, and called to serve,
She keeps her poise, never unnerved.
   Cindy Winstead's one of a kind,
   Who's pleasant and blessed with a mind.
   That's sharp and swift to speak the Word,
   "In season" so it will be "heard."
O' fathomless the wealth should start,
As this dear woman shares her heart.
The aspirant smell of success,
Drifts down to her while she's addressed...
   "Well done! My faithful lovely one,
   Your works concur with My Son!
   The prayers you've aired are manifest,
   So enter now unto My rest:
Fellowship with Me, My child,
For I'll be with you all the while!"

DESTINY'S SONG

The ardent zeal God's "Temple" feels,
When columns hail, "rejoice."
Are vaulted archway's vital display,
Of "Praise" crescendos voiced!
 A Victor's Triumphful Entry,
 Slams still the *foes* advance;
 For God ordained His men to sing,
 And Worship Him in dance!
Euphoric chants of "Jesus, Lord,"
Attract the passerby;
While signs and wonders manifest,
Each one to testify.
 The Healer, Savior, Son of God,
 Has come in man to dwell.
 E'en through God's Grace and Written Word,
 He enters those we tell.
Why think on things of the past,
When "NOW" salvation is;
The essence of our very life,
To be "Born" into "His."
 Perfect and without blemish,
 Before our King we stand;
 So boldly in His presence,
 To grasp our Brother's hand.
'Cause never will He leave us,
Our song exalts His Name;
The "One" Who's given "All" for us,
Where others we may claim.
 And lead them to *His Kingdom*,
 Beyond all Earth's sorrow;
 So Heaven's Gate they may relate,
 Their destiny's tomorrow.

SHE'S "SEW" FINE

Bernadette, the stars should let,
Their beams come from "Your eyes";
With glistened rays to break the haze,
Of darkness in the skies!
    Your countenance, aglow with love,
    Received o'er every look;
    Opens pages laced by Grace,
    Written in God's Book.
That's more than just a manual,
Crammed full of do's and don'ts;
For when you *love*, you'll only see,
"His desire" your wants.
    Your gentle heart mends the tear,
    Others felt when "rent";
    While Jesus *sews* that heart through you,
    By *mercy* He has sent!
This "stitch" entwined has lent her time,
To meet her brother's need;
As need'les" produce holes to fill,
Adjoined when *seams* succeed.

    Her kindness sown shall be reaped,
    In every detail;
    A "Harvest" filled with fruits of Joy,
    From "prayers" which do "avail."
Lead on! King Jesus though this maid,
Your beauty and splendor;
Upon the brooks of life we walk,
To meet the ones she's for!

OUR FATHER'S WILL

Sing unto the Lord, ye earth,
And show forth day to day;
His salvation's glorious,
O' to the heathen say,
    "Great is our Lord and His works,
    Forever to be praised.
    Above all gods and images,
    Which lowly men have made!"
Our God has made the Heavens,
All honor and strength give place;
Before Him Glory due His name,
Stand up! Ye human race.
    Let oceans roar and fields rejoice,
    With all that is therein:
    While trees cry out, "His Presence,
    E'en stones can't but proclaim:
"Blessed be our God and King,
"Whose mercy never ends!"
Oh, shout out Saints, "His Goodness,
In Grace to us descend!"
    Keep mindful of the covenant;
    Our master has conveyed;
    That whosoever calls on Him,
    By His Son shall be saved.
Though Jesus crucified and died,
Then by God's Power raised;
Breaking chains of death and hell,
And we can't seem to Praise?
    The One who took our sin and strife,
    And poverty away;
    To give us life, health, peace and joy,
    With righteousness to pray.

"Father, we come boldly,
Expectantly to see:
"Your willingness enacted,
To meet our every need!"

TAMARA

The heir to Praise chose Tamara,
Though by his father's hand;
While wickedness stayed in his midst,
He left his wife barren.
    Trying to cope with no hope,
    The brother 'twas to raise;
    Seed to breed, but only grieved,
    The Lord to end his days.
Judah felt his last son's help,
To carry on his name;
Might be replaced by his decease,
So he made them refrain.
    But Tamara had a promise,
    According to the law;
    That she'd indeed bear that seed,
    Descendants would talk of.
From Ruth the Moabites,
Via lineage of our Lord;
Would all acclaim, that their fame,
Was made because the Word.
    Became the Life that's in It,
    While acted on when heard;
    Not just a little promise,
    That's easily deterred!
Do we deceive ourselves or God,
When we neglect 'twas done;
Two thousand years ago you know,
By His Beloved Son?
    Awake unto His Righteousness,
    And *Rise* to meet God's call;
    To save, heal, and deliver,
    Those broken from the Fall!

Resurrection Power,
Christ Blood, and e'en His name;
Are given us to bring the lost,
Back in the fold again!
    Put on your armor Kings and Priest,
    The battle cry is nigh;
    So fight with might till our Lord,
    Splits forth that eastern sky!

Genesis 38; Luke 3:33; Ruth 4:12

THE FEELING OF BEING FELT

Oh, my soul doth cry out,
The pain we have been through;
From lack of understanding,
The "Body" we're made to.
 Be a part and prompt its growth,
 Yet often times may stunt;
 While sharpening against one's Grain,
 "Our point" became quite blunt!
When we can feel for others,
The way which Jesus did;
We'll keep our tongues from wagging,
O'er things that others said.
 Majoring on minors,
 Is often thought to cause;
 Righteous indignation,
 Toward men who've made the flaws.
How our wives felt, we'd have knelt,
And prayed the Lord to see;
Their concern that we learn,
How to meet their need!
 Our touch is more than a grasp,
 To fill a sensual fire;
 But rather loving hands and heart,
 That proclaims our desire!
Expressions of charisma,
We're "noted" to convey;
So why the inhibition,
In calling those who stray.
 And leave the "flock" for fellowship,
 They didn't seem to find;
 Because our "cliques" didn't mix,
 Nor try to find the time?

The book of Life is where our Lord,
Wrote how we did gather;
And speak of Him and what *He'd* done,
Not "Shield Shows" to confer.
    Let's once again be a friend,
    To those who are without;
    By adding works to our faith,
    And shedding fear and doubt.
That we might lose our place in line,
When the Rapture comes;
But rather hear from our Lord,
"Good job, My Son, well done!"
    "As much as ye have done it
    Unto the least of these,
    My Brethren, ye have done it,
    Not to them, but Me, Jesus." (Matthew 25:40)

Malachi 3:16-18; 1 Peter 3:7-12; Galatians 5:13-26; Mark 9:39-42; Luke 6:31; 36-38;

1 John 3:16-24.

SPRING FEVER

The fluttering of meadowlarks,
While squirrels chat their song;
Keeps the rhythm of Spring,
Going right along!
    Bumblebees make pollen sprees,
    In blossom's dust of yellow;
    As they all share the year's first warm air,
    With spirit's light and mellow.
Lover's leap their heart's a fleet,
Like dandelions swift of wind;
O'er timeless dreams they shall glean,
So precious in their mind!
    Their fragrant prayers go to share,
    The love which they have found;
    Soaring to our Father's ear,
    Stemming from their heart's ground.
Motionless their gaze fulfills,
A look of peace and joy;
With eyes comprised of contentment,
And harmony deployed.
    O' the royal colors shown,
    In gold of daffodils;
    Or purple thrift and irises,
    Stretched across the hills.
The crimson tulip's bright array,
Drapes the fields that dogwoods shield;
O'er a row where pansies grow,
By the pomp crepe myrtles yield.
    See the glory God's conveyed,
    In blessing us by what He's made;
    And consider how this bliss,
    Is typified by morning mist.

Praise Him for all He has given,
Expressly in the life we're livin'.
Thank God for your helpmeet dear,
And ever hold her to you near!

EULOGY TO A FRIEND

To Emory Brown, his body down,
But spirit lifted up;
Though graduating early,
His life's end seemed abrupt!
   While memories to us will mean,
   Thoughts we all can cherish;
   May we think on lives he touched,
   By "Him" whose touch first made us.
Brownie's love for rocks and gems,
Showed the quality of him;
Shined and polished, most dignified,
Yet a man with feelings, cried.
   Our loss might seem a fleeting sway,
   Of heartache though we truly say;
   "There's no remorse for those whose choice,
   Has been set on Heaven's course!"
We loved this man and will take note,
How he liked to prod and poke;
A little laughter at ourselves,
And see our candor is not to shelf!
   His honesty and heart to please,
   Led him to give beyond his need;
   Should not a life expressed as this,
   Be more than just a farewell kiss?
For what we do to others makes,
A motive that the Lord can take;
And write within His Book of Life,
He chose reward instead of strife.
   Brownie's gone, but not forlorn,
   'Cause soon we'll see the Lord's return;
   And rise our bodies to unite,
   With other souls who make the flight.

Let's remain enriched to know,
There's more to life than what we show;
And thank God for the very ground,
Of hearts made fertile by Emory brown.

MY CROWN

She loves the Lord with all her heart,
A student of His Word;
Keeping her body under,
A "temple" that's preserved.
    By staying fit, trim, and in shape,
    Devout strength she puts on;
    With spiritual adorning,
    And honor to be worn!
A pleasant, godly countenance,
Bears eyes that show wisdom;
Along with hands industrious,
Not idle to become!
    Her tongue is one to follow,
    The law that kindness curves;
    Whereby her gentle spirit,
    Flows out those winsome words.
Which Jesus speaks out to her,
Upon her early rise;
Of prayer to hear what's dear and near,
Her Lord's will comprise.
    E'er patient and longsuffering,
    Whose trust is ne'er a lack;
    Because her heart's entwined with His,
    So faith comes to react.
In fertile soil you need not toil,
For "its" been tilled by love;
Wherein this "blend" is Heaven sent,
Received from *Whom* it's of!
    May this blessing be to me,
    An aspiration given;
    Of Life's essence and Beauty,
    Through Jesus Christ: the "Risen."

IF WE PROVOKE OUR YOKE, WE'RE BROKE

Come to Me, Jim Munsey,
With your wife, Carolyn;
And link your obligation,
So I can oblige mine!
    I've made ya'll to be fires,
    But I provide the flame;
    Kindled by obedience,
    Adherent of My Name!
My pleasure you've provided,
While waiting on My voice;
Disciplined, you planned to win,
Because you've made the choice.
    Of excellence in ministry,
    To train My Blessed lambs;
    Whereby the *Word* that they've heard,
    Will conquer many lands.
Yet unseen but often dreamed,
My Power shall reveal;
Our manifested Glory,
As thousands *shall* be healed!
    I love you, Jim and Carolyn,
    Be faithful evermore;
    And you'll increase that fire,
    With Words that will implore.
The hearts of men to feel that zeal,
And LINK as you did Me;
To win the lost whate'er the cost $,
Then set the captives Free!!

Psalm 103:21; 104:4; Matthew 11:28; John 21:15; II Corinthians 3:6-12; 6:4; Mark
11:24; 1 John 5.

153

THE TEACHER

Lucy, you see, a student
Is one which can be taught;
"Principles" of learning,
Are worth the time they cost!
    How often we're told to grow,
    From experience;
    Then left a dangling question mark,
    In quest of common sense.
Countless ways wisdom's conveyed,
Apparently it's shown;
Though without application,
It wistfully is gone.
    Be swift to hear and slow to speak,
    Till registered in mind;
    For that computes upon your heart,
    A vault unleashed which finds.
A plan that coincides,
With God when He's sought first;
And not just sensual intellect,
Amassed from a quick burst.
    Of words which can be piercing,
    Lest tempered by our Lord;
    And cut the very souls of men,
    If negligently we have heard.
It's said we use but a tenth,
Of the mind we're given;
But the rest is still at work,
Digesting what's been fed in.
    The light shines o'er those little ones,
    As they each comprehend;
    Revelations to their mind,
    Whose messages will send.

Knowledge of their Maker,
Who bowed to reach His man;
And give the "Very Essence,"
Of Life's Eternal Plan.
    Man quotes to have such wisdom,
    But omits the very One;
    Who calculates the ocean's weight,
    Within His mighty palm.
Then takes the dust upon a scale,
To measure mountains, hill, and vale;
Our God who spanned the Universe,
And gave His Son to break the curse!
    The fragrant aroma God's chosen,
    In herbs that fill the air;
    Is just a scant example,
    Of how for man He cares.
He clothes the fields which bountifully yield,
Sustenance to eat;
And says, "You go proclaim My Love,
And I'll supply your need!"
    May we in studies truly learn,
    Never from God to ever turn;
    But see His Word's our will indeed,
    For then we really can succeed!

Psalm 119:130; Proverbs 2:1-11; 3:1-11; 4:18-24; 28:5; Isaiah 40:12; Matthew 7:24;

1 Corinthians 2:4-16; James 1; 3:9-18; II Timothy 3:15-17.

THE WELLSPRING OF LIFE

Many be called yet have not chosen,
The purpose of their lives;
Keeping most gifts and talents,
Imbedded deep inside.
 One saint whose name is Rebekah,
 Typified it best;
 When her gift of faithfulness,
 Brought favor to be blessed!
How many times we pass the time,
When opportunities arise;
Where our "fruit" could produce,
Some "Hope" in other's lives!
 Rebekah sought obedience,
 Her guideline to secure;
 The actions which she made,
 Would "prove" her heart was pure!
Precious gold symbolized,
Her works tried as by fire;
While "joy" to please her Lord,
Caused fathomless desire!
 Who would've thought a camel maid,
 Could land into this wealth?
 Through the earth God hath promised,
 The "meek" who trust not self.
But totally depend on Him,
For "the union" dues He's paid;
So our Father can bestow,
"All" He has ever made!
 God gave His Son to make us one,
 And legally be free;
 From sin, death, hate, and sin's fate,
 Then leaves the "choice" to me!

O' call upon Jesus as Lord,
And give your life to God;
Seeking as Rebekah,
Reception of His Love!

Genesis 23; Matthew 20:16; 22:14; 5:3-16; Psalm 37:3-6; 1 Corinthians 12; 3:13-16; 13;

Galatians 5:22-25; Proverbs 18:4, 16; II Timothy 1:6; 1 Peter 1:22; 4:10.

RACHAEL

Jacob's ladder left to him,
A state of ecstasy;
Seeing beyond the natural realm,
Into the Spirit's degree!
    His promises were enhanced,
    Upon the land of Haran;
    As to the well, he met Rachael,
    And showed his strength 'twas awesome.
"He" rolled the stone and made it known,
"Her" beauty was impressive;
While romance began to dance,
He knew his heart's conclusive.
    His mother too was from a well,
    "Met" towards matrimony;
    While God's plan began to span,
    A union and his family.
O' Jacob thou hadst found thy love,
In this Jewish maid;
While seven years you served for her,
Seemed only a few days!
    Your mother well had taught you,
    How diligence should strive;
    Though the ways don't justify,
    The means that oft' arrive!
You tricked your brother Esau,
As you deceived your dad;
When you connived in that lie,
To get what he should've had.
    Now, this blessed' Rachael,
    Your heart goes out to wed;
    Then morningtime you should find,
    "Deceit" has come instead.

What God hath promised He'll fulfill,
But our lives must yield our will;
Wherein His Word we concur,
By "acting on" what we have heard!
    Jacob's wives still conceived,
    Israel's house toward "Promised Seed";
    Rachael though had many doubts,
    For, from her womb, it seemed left out.
Should we not see how too our dreams,
Seem blocked from their fruition;
By having "Trust" begin to "Rust"
From "airs" of wrong decisions.
    God sets before us life and death,
    A blessing or a curse;
    Then encourages His Ways, not ours,
    We choose to seek them first.
O man, do you now see what's good,
And required of thee?
How justice finds God's mercy,
In love to walk humbly.
    Totally dependent,
    On Him who first loved us;
    So hopeless cares don't bring despair,
    But gleaming rays of trust.
Are your visions tunneled,
Or panoramic view;
Because God's Power's channeled,
In vessels He works through!

Genesis 28; 29; 35:2, 10-11; Ruth 4:11; Micah 6:8; Deuteronomy 30; Matthew 6:31-34.

THE CURSE REVERSED

The harmony in God's whole scheme,
Of Redemption is:
How Calvary won for me,
All that Jesus did!
    Our Lord had won the opposites,
    Of all which He had suffered;
    Giving us Life in His death,
    Then health from stripes which tortured.
The curse He bore so we'd be blessed,
Thus giving us His Righteousness;
Chastised for our Peace of mind,
And bound to free all mankind!
    As a Lamb, He stood silent,
    Thus making for our rights;
    To proclaim His glorious Name,
    Where darkness bows to Light!
Poverty He took to be,
And made me rich in Him;
But most of all, He gave His all,
Completing Salvation.
    God asked that we bear Him fruit,
    Which shows what he has done;
    Letting His Love in us Shine,
    And magnify His Son!
Too little too late won't elate,
Our call to spread His Word;
So be "doers" of what you've learned,
Not hearers that just heard!

"WELL DONE"

The love of God shed in our heart
Has called to *gather,* NOT to *part!*
The Holy Spirit baptized me,
And through the Word, set me free.
    Yet only freedom don't pursue,
    Without releasing captives too.
    For what we do to others makes,
    A motive that the Lord can take.
And write within His Book of Life,
He chose "*reward!*" instead of *strife!*
Our coming Savior does "Rejoice,"
To hear *no* murmur, but the voice
    Of faithful, fruitful, Saints alike,
    Who spread "Good News" in love and might.
    "Well done!" we hear from the "Most High,"
    As we spurt forth into the sky.

Tune: "A Mighty Fortress Is Our God"

Romans 5:5; Ephesians 6:8; Philippians 2:14; Luke 19:17; 1 Thessalonians 5:13; 4:17.

MY DEAR WIFE

Your sandy-blonde hair of smooth texture,
Flows o'er your soft fawn skin;
With crystal blue eyes as the skies,
So deep I may gaze in.
 And see the hope and image,
 You made before our God;
 That this day you would say,
 "I've *now* found my true Love!"
Your voice is kind and gentle,
Yet sings crescendos praise;
Amid a nose so sleek and pretty,
Never haughtily is raised.
 Your physique and body typifies,
 God's handiwork conceived;
 Perfection in its balance,
 In tone as that of Eve!
Affectionate lips and ivory teeth,
Discreetly kept by dimple cheeks;
Your smile implores tranquility,
Then exuberance to excite me!
 Five foot five your stature stands,
 By legs as arches built;
 Strong and well designed for you're
 Running to stay fit.
The countenance you express,
Keeps my heartbeat at its best!
Your beauty complements us both,
And makes our union give others hope!
 Jesus sparkles through your eyes,
 And draws me unto you;
 O may our lives exemplify,
 The Power God will do.

In two who have become one,
And joined to glorify His Son!
Having prayers go to the tenth,
Building our family's inner strength!
    Our talents, desires, and love abound,
    And minister to others;
    Overcoming problems,
    And things that try to bother:
The Gospel *we're* called to spread,
Giving "life" to all that's dead;
Healing bodies and marriages,
Sharing our rights and privileges;
    God's given us to enjoy,
    As His Word we deploy!

IS THE SON IN YOUR EYES?

The Heavens are telling of
The Glory due our God.
Their vast expanse so declare,
His Handiwork that's awed!
    Sunset skies do typify
    All Majesty unfurled.
    And God's Peace amidst the sea
    Of People in this world.
The Firmament is "Beauty,"
Personified by God!
Though men may think, "A Pretty Scene,"
It's "Him" we Praise and Laud!
    We adjure our lives and hearts,
    Responsive to his Grace;
    And give Thanks to the Most High,
    Uplifted hands and face.
Toward Heavenward we look up,
At Him Who *first* looked down.
Oh, Bless the Lord and be still,
And know that He's around!
    Omnipotence and All Love's,
    Not slack and doesn't leave;
    All creation testifies,
    Why then can't man believe?
There is a God and purpose,
Beyond all this splendor;
He is Christ, Who gives us Life,
'Cause our sins He died for!
    Again the sky is lowering,
    To draw another day;
    May we reach those to Jesus,
    Who keeps us as we pray.

They will be done in Heaven,
And on the Earth as well;
To bring us to Your Kingdom,
And others that will tell!

Psalm 19:1; 45:3-4;46:10; 63:1-8; Jude 24, 25; Ephesians 1:2-3; 1 Corinthians 15:57;

1 John 4:19; 5:9-15; Hebrews 13:5; Luke 11:2-4; Mark 16:15-20.

THE ROSE OF SHARON

(Song of Solomon)

As a rose may grow,
So does Love.
Both their beauty unending…

But remember this,
Seek God's bliss.
For there is "time" worth spending!
For there is time worth spending!…

Its petals of Love,
Draw the Son,
Witnessing to Beholders…

Aspiring all of them,
Unto "Him."
"New Life" that last forever!
New Life that lasts forever!…

POWER OF PRAISE

Praise the Lord from the Heavens,
Oh, Praise Him in the heights.
Praise Him all ye His angels,
Sun, moon and stars of Light!
 Praise Him created waters,
 And clap to Him in waves.
 All cattle, birds, and creatures,
 It's "His Name" that we raise!
Oh, lightning, hail, fog and frost,
And stormy winds fulfill.
Orders sent out from the Lord,
Then bow the trees and hill!
 Kings and Princes and Judges,
 Both young men and maidens.
 Exalt and glorify our God,
 Whose Majesty's Supreme!
He's lifted up for His own,
All power to prosper.
Though benefits are not *drawn*,
When we do not *draw* near!

Psalm 148; 92:1-5; 89:16-17; 75:10; Acts 2:38-39; Ephesians 2:17; Hebrews 13:15;

Isaiah 57:19.

GOD'S WAVELENGTH

The symmetry of ocean tide,
Subsiding to her source;
Can't help but make the "Hidden Eye,"
Ponder upon their force,
Serene and yet still mighty,
The crashing waves' white foam;
Beckons to its listeners,
"We welcome you back home." (chorus)

Come ye heavy laden,
Into His Sea of Grace;
And let your sins be washed and cleansed,
No more to be retraced!
A crystal sea awaits us,
With Rainbow o'er the throne;
And "covenant" of peace Procured,
To whom the Son makes known. (repeat)
They listened, loved and trusted Me,
To God he will thus say,
So enter in My children,
All Heaven is your stay!

Chorus: Messiah's second coming,
Will be for those He died:
Rejoicing or a grieving,
A moaning or a sign!

Tune: "Ghost Rider in the Sky"

Psalm 107; 104; Matthew 11:28; 25:34; Romans 5:1.

OF HEAVEN SO FAIR,

The New Song in Our Heart

Jesus, You are drawing nigh,
In the clouds with great glory.
We patiently wait Your soon return,
You are Lord and all knees shall bow.
 Even so, Come quickly, Lord,
 For Your "Bride" who's ready to go.
 The gates of Heaven break open wide,
 God and man are now unified!
Holy Spirit indwell my soul,
Teach me everything I should know.
Encompass me with God's Truth and Love,
Till we reign with Him from above!
 Are you goin' to heaven so fair?
 Angels praise and worship Him there;
 How beautiful are the streets of gold,
 Mansions built our Savior foretold.

Music from: "Scarborough Fair," by Paul Simon and Art Garfunkel.

SOUL CONTROL

Be not conformed to this world,
But transformed in your mind;
Renewing it through God's Word,
Then wisdom you will find!
    Keep a guard upon your heart,
    For out of it will flow;
    Issues of "Living Water,"
    Eternal "fruit" to grow.
Your abiding in the Vine,
Means more than just "*hang loose*";
For fruitless limbs are cut down,
Because they have no use.
    Let's live our lives for the Lord,
    In His capacity;
    And don't box in our vision,
    Of setting all men free.
From fear, doubt, hate and sin's fate,
We must draw on God's Grace;
And start within each one of them,
God's love to put in place!
    Gird up, grow up and go forth,
    Proclaiming Jesus Christ;
    And His Good News don't refuse,
    But pay the "highest price."
For no man has given up,
Marriage, folks, or home;
Yet he'll receive, in this life,
A hundredfold return!
    May our conversation be,
    In truth apart from strife;
    Speaking, "God's among us,"
    The Glory of our Life!

Depart from unforgiveness,
As martyr's dying plea;
"Father, please forgive them,
For this their wicked deed!"
    Vengeance is God's and He'll "repay,"
    But what we "owe" is Love;
    So render this on your list,
    Of "mandates" to think of!

Romans 12; 13:8-14; Proverbs 4:20-29; Jude 21; Mark 10:28-29; James 3:9-18; John 15:1-18; Acts 7:60.

A PROPOSED PROPOSAL

Oh, Dear One, Your eyes so True,
Set sail within my heart;
A longing love that will flow,
And can't ever depart.
    From its Source that's been well sought,
    O'er faith in prayer for you;
    My God told me that I'd see,
    The "favor" that He'll do.
In blessing me way beyond,
All Heaven would have shown;
For you are the Gift of Love,
That's seen because it's Known.
    By a color that won't fade,
    Nor bleach out life with strife;
    'Cause you fill in every sense,
    My glory and my life!
I've waited long but my prayers;
Were heard right from the first;
And so, I ask you for Your hand,
In mine that we might burst.
    Into a life, that was meant,
    Our Savior did foresee;
    Us one with Him Who is Love,
    And wills that we be free.
To share the goals of our souls,
And interest conveyed;
Oh, "Praise the Lord!" for bringing,
Our paths to cross that day!
    Should you be the one for me,
    This witness will be true;
    If no peace, your spirit sees,
    Then "God's Choice" let us do.

THE TIMELESS WEDDING

This marriage feast now begins,
An appetite whereof,
Each other does not exist,
To fill your mate with love.
    God formed man up from the dust,
    And saw what he needed,
    Her name was Eve and how she,
    Made Adam completed!
Oh, dignity and honor,
A wife brings to her man,
As he does love and cherish,
In God's perfected plan.
    Though physically the *weaker*,
    Your union is not *less*,
    You serve and do defend her,
    And can't wait to caress.
The beautiful and gentle,
"One" that means all to you,
Whose calm dawn eyes bring reply,
"Whatever can I do?"
    As she serves unto the Lord,
    Subjected is his wife,
    Treats him with such compassion,
    Washed in the "Word of Life!"
No man can put asunder,
What God has joined as "one,"
With him, His Son, and Spirit,
And "Power" that's begun.
    In prayers that *do* avail much,
    To make the devil flee,
    Ten times he runs the faster,
    And wishes he'd never see.

The "covenant" that you made,
With Jesus Christ Your King,
And lives that *will* be enhanced,
So God can truly bring.
    A family made of *love*,
    Their sin covered over,
    By "one" who said, "He'd remain!"
    'Cause He cannot falter.
May your prosper and increase,
God's wisdom to *attain*;
And remember your First Love!
Will always stay the *same*.
    God does have the best for you,
    If "only" we will live,
    For the Lord and put our trust,
    In "Him" who wants to give! Amen.

Genesis 1:26; 2:7-25; Psalm 105:4; Proverb 18:22; 31:10-31; Song of Solomon;

Mark 10:9; 1 Corinthians 11:7; Ephesians 5:15-33; Colossians 3:17-19; 1 Peter 3:7.

THE LEGAL EAGLE

We gratefully
Do praise the Lord,
And laud and magnify
   The "One" Who heals
   And will forgive,
   As well as satisfy.
Our want and need
And Youth renewed,
Like Eagles sure and strong!
   But may we keep
   What He's entrust;
   His "Benefits" be known,
For gifts that are
Never received
Are not classed as our own!
   How unused strength
   Is like a dream
   That never is conveyed.
And direction
For all our life
Should we have *never* prayed!
   Oh, Eagle Soar
   And lock your wings;
   Through storm and tempest fly.
Above the clouds,
That are in our life,
By Jesus Christ on high!

Psalm 103:1-5: Isaiah 40:31; Job 39:26-29; Obadiah 4: James 4:3.

FROM HEAVEN'S WARD
(MATERNITY THAT IS)

Unto You is born this day,
A beautiful daughter.
Love embraced a new mom's arms,
Compares but to her father!
    A "gift of God" given you,
    Is joyously received;
    For you stood upon His Word,
    And got what you believed.
Dimple smile and mother's eyes,
Will never you forget;
Nor the "Promise" from the Lord,
Our "need" is always met!
    Cherishing that little one,
    To whom you both shall train;
    To know the "Word" and love God,
    And realize "He's" the same.
"One" that brought her to this world,
And keeps her day by day;
Nurtured, healthy, and complete,
To where she can't but say:
    "I love my folks who gave me,
    The opportune to live;
    And My Lord Jesus Christ,
    Who 'wills' to save and give."
Another "Life" that won't end,
'Cause time is then erased;
So I "Praise Him" night and day,
And thank God for His grace!

Psalm 22:10; 127:3-5; 128:1-6; 147:11-14; 103:17; James 1:17; Mark 11:23; Ephesians

6:13-14; 6:24; 1:7; 2:8; Deuteronomy 28:1-4; 30:19; Proverbs 17:6; 22:6; Philippians

4:19; John 14:21; Romans 2:7.

FIT TO USE

God tempts no man to evil do,
Yet trials still do arise;
His opportunes are not a few,
And they are no disguise.
Because the heart is what He tests,
To let our faith show through;
And all in all, God wants the "best,"
But we must deem to choose!

James 1:13; Deuteronomy 33:19; Malachi 3:3.

GOD'S C.A.R.E. PACKAGE

Don't worry 'bout tomorrow,
But live from day to day;
'Cause worry's interest,
On "Debts" you must not pay!
    Our life is but a vapor,
    It leaves and doesn't stay;
    Therefore we seek a Savior,
    Who's Christ, the only Way!
He'll not forsake nor leave you,
With anxious thoughts or care;
For "burdens" are His business,
Each one He loves to bear!
    Come close to Him and you'll see,
    Your griefs turn into joy;
    And a peace that doesn't cease,
    All this He does employ.
To bless and keep His children,
In order to restore;
Them through their faith and meekness,
So we can love "Him" more!

James 4:8, 14; 1:21; Philippians 4:6-8; Psalm 23:3; Isaiah 51:11; Matthew 11:28-30.

WATCH THEM "WILEY" WEEDS

(That Choke the Word Out of One's LIFE!*)*

As fire and smoke may burn and choke,
So does lust conceive;
And worldly care will bring despair,
To those who don't believe.
    Jesus Christ, Our Lord has died,
    So that we might live;
    Why then must we rob and steal?
    When we're called to give!
Bless the needy, poor, and lame,
Through the Grace that's in ya;
And the Lord will make of you,
A vessel to contin-yah'.
    Then we'll meet Him in the sky,
    Eternity is laden;
    Well done! Now my little child,
    Come on into Heaven!
What He is to you is shown,
In what you do to others,
So let us live unto Jesus,
Who is our Big Brother!

WHEREIN LIES THE "VICTORY?"

What's in our sight,
Is not the fight;
But *Spiritual* endeavors.
　　Our Holy Lord,
　　Provides His Word;
　　A "*Sword*" which quickly severs.
Faith instilled,
And Spirit-filled;
We *go undaunted* warriors.
　　The battle won,
　　We've just begun;
　　To *see* whose side we're fightin'.
Yet what you know,
Is not enough;
For skirmishes with Satan.
　　'Cause what you do,
　　Will tell on you;
　　If *"you"* are who you're servin'.
All the talk,
And none the walk;
No *victory* will be seeded.
　　But if the heart,
　　Is where you start;
　　Your quest is near completed.
For in the Name,
Of Jesus Christ;
All enemies defeated.

John 16:14-15; Ephesians 6:11, 15.

TO MOM

My love for you is more than
A casual reply.
For it's meant to be well sent,
Until the day I die.
    No gratitude can measure,
    The things you've brought me through.
    So, this day I celebrate,
    And look toward what to do;
To lift your life and Spirit,
O'er elements and time.
Then rejoice with you, Dear Mom,
And thank you God that you're mine.
    I know your kindness sowed,
    In me a field of love;
    And good fruit to bless you,
    Each time I think thereof!

DAD'S DELIGHTFUL DAY

Dad, you've meant the most to me,
In words which little tell;
How to express, "You're the best!"
No motto must I sell.
    For in excellence and Truth,
    My life's been geared by you;
    To see the right in His might,
    And make a point to do,
What's pleasing and in order,
So as to please my Dad.
Though times gone past, I've been rasp,
Not seeing what I had;
    To draw in your future plan;
    Toward making me a man.
    And promote your thoughts, not mine,
    Obeying as I can!
You reserve a special place,
Which can't be bought or sold;
'Cause from my heart where wealth starts,
My love to you unfolds!

Exodus 20:12; Proverbs 4:1-8; 10:1; 15:20; 23:22-29; Luke 6:36; 11:11-13; 15:12-29;

Ephesians 6:1-4; Colossians 3:20.

LAODICEANS (*LAY OFF THE SINS*)

So many in that day,
Shall come to Him and say,
"Lord, Lord! It is but us,
The ones You really trust!"
    Yet from the voice of truth,
    They hear His still refute,
    "No, never did I know,
    Your works you claim to show.
'Cause I looked at your heart,
Which you held far apart.
Though once I entered in,
You stayed a 'distant friend'!"
    A *boxed-in* worship hour,
    Denied you of My Power,
    And those "doctrines of men,"
    Destroyed your lives *within*!
Forsake all but leaving none,
Thus you left My work undone.
Heal the sick and raise the dead,
All just *talk* is what you said.
    Hungry, naked, and destitute,
    To these you gave your reproof,
    "It's *our church* they must attend,"
    But not a dollar did you lend!
I spew you out of My mouth,
And call those who ran the route.
Of Love, Joy, Peace and Patience,
Self-control and Faithfulness.
    To serve Me and their fellow man,
    And ever lend a helping hand.
    In spreading Jesus and "His Worth,"
    That He died for our "New Birth."

And in His Kingdom they shall dwell,
But as for you, yours will be _____?
Dear Friend, it's up to you.

Revelation 3:14-22; Psalm 50:16-23; Matthew 25:31-46; Mark 1:15; 4:24; 6:6-23;

10:29-30; 16:15-20; Luke 6:35-38; 45-49; 8:15; 9:1; 10:1-9; 1 Timothy 2:15-26; 3:1-7;

Galatians 5:14-26; 6:1-2; Ephesians 4:23-32; II Peter 1:1-11.

THINK ON THESE THINGS

"Evil thoughts!" I bind you up,
And cast away the key;
For Jesus is My "Main Wave,"
That crashes in the sea.
    Of memories which can be no more,
    Washed in His cleansing Blood;
    Though enemy may come in,
    A standard is God's flood.
His Spirit living in us,
To guide our lives aright;
And the Word which enters in,
Will make God's Truth the Light!
    Let none of you imagine,
    An evil in your heart;
    Nor any lie which will die,
    To keep you far apart.
From the throne and answers known,
God needs you turned to Him;
To "polish up" your life in Love,
He seeks His "Precious Gem!"
    Be not wise in your own eyes,
    But trusting in the Lord;
    For "deception's" cost is great,
    More than you can afford!
Be not moved by what you see,
Nor even what you feel;
But rather "STAND" on God's Word,
Which always makes it "real!"
    Streams of life flow in your veins,
    And to your heart renew;

Christ is at a two-way door,
All we must do is choose!

Proverbs 23:7; 4:23; II Corinthians 10:5; 5:7; 17; Philippians 4:8-19; Psalm

103:12; 101:3; 119:130; 66:18; Isaiah 59:19; 1 Timothy 6:4; Zechariah 8:16-17;

1 Peter 1:7; 1 Corinthians 15:33; Deuteronomy 30:19; John 10:9-11.

THE ANOINTED SECRETARY

May you be blessed
With Heaven's best;
Of every perfect gift
And love Divine.
Which does entwine
Each other to uplift;
You're one who will
Be quiet and still.
To hear your brother's need
And see the job;
Is "unto God"!
Whereby it does succeed!

SEED INDEED

To God I sow,
And spread His Son;
A message till,
His Kingdom come!
As we all wait,
Upon the Lord;
His loving Grace,
Grows more and more.
And though the fight,
May seem bitter;
Our loving God,
Raised no "quitter!"

GOD'S WORKMANSHIP

To John Layton, man of God,
Who's faithful, pure and just;
Like his God, of Whom he serves,
Apart from guile or lust!
    How inspiring is this man,
    That seeks the Lord each day;
    In business deals and at home,
    God's Spirit leads his way!
Jehovah's given to John,
A love to meet man's needs;
Through council and well-seasoned words,
"In tune" he intercedes.
    To bring God's blessings upon,
    All those he comes to know;
    And instructions in the path,
    Of faith and love we go!
Jesus' body, all are we,
To operate in line;
As for John, he would be one,
Classed in that of the spine!
    For spiritual fortitude,
    Is needful to compose;
    A warrior fit for battle,
    Believing "Whom" he knows.
Will bring him to the summit,
Defeating all his foes;
Though time and strength want to gain,
In poverty and woes.
    All victory in Jesus,
    Surrounds this man of Hope;
    No "shoe string faith" ties his fate,
    But that of tensile Rope.

May God work "Big" in this man,
To let his light so shine;
In a Radiance of Love,
Which truly is Divine!

Ephesians 2:10; Proverbs 28:20; 23:19; Psalm 112:5; 1 Peter 2:1, 21-22; Isaiah 64:5;

Colossians 1: 17-19; Acts 2:33-36; Romans 4:20-21; Hebrews 3:6; Matthew 5:16.

THE ADVENT OF OUR KING

Peace, good will toward men, they say,
Jesus, our Lord was born this day.
A host of angels praise His Name!
And, we too, should do the same.
    Emmanuel, God with us,
    All glory to the Babe born just!
    Our Counselor and Prince of Peace,
    The Son of God who set us free.
No more a curse in sin's domain,
But "saved" by Him to rule and reign!
O'er Satan and his hell-bent throng,
It's God's power that's made us strong.
    We celebrate the "Babe" 'twas born,
    But let us look to *His* return.
    May the joy of the Lord,
    This season come,
Seeing the good things,
That He has done.
For Christ came to this world,
That we might *live*,
    So let's follow Him,
    To love and to give!

SHOE STRING FAITH

Shoe String Faith is that which needs,
Someone to keep it "tied."
Though the "sole" is safe and sure,
It breaks whenever tried!
    Usually when strings are loose,
    The "tongue" flops open wide;
    And all our help to replace,
    Is hindered by their "pride"!
It's earmarked by the "Highest Name,"
A shoe string can attain;
And a "Lifetime Guarantee,"
So, who then is to blame?
    When wear and tear brings despair,
    To those who 'dorn this faith;
    Or stumble from outstretched loops,
    And quit when they should break.
We all are told to stand firm.
Whatever be the cost;
'Cause God redeems those torn strings,
And finds them when they're lost!
    Keep taut the Faith!

GOD'S FRANCHISE

Fran, Dear Saint, your countenance,
Implores tranquility;
Amidst all trials and darts of doubt,
You laugh with childlike glee.
    Her fadeless grin evolves within,
    A heart made of pure gold!
    Nor broken spirit, but that of joy,
    Repels all earth's sorrow.
Peace, love, joy long suffering's,
Depicted by her face;
And as "praises" still satan,
"No Way" to give him place!
    Through God's word and gentle smile,
    The thoughtfulness that's brought;
    "New Life" and a restored faith,
    When Jesus' love is wrought.
No downcast frown shall touch the ground,
This spirit tilled with love;
For *in* trials, she breaks that smile,
And thanks her God above!
    Exhorting and uplifting,
    Encouragement she sees;
    As a witness to win souls,
    And heal the ones in need!
Her "light's" illuminating,
Enduring and self-*less*;
To seek and save them that's lost,
And lead them to His rest!

Numbers 6:25-26; Psalm 16:8-11; 4:6; 11:7; 42:5; 90:8; Proverbs 12:25; 15:13; 17:22;

29:10; Acts 2:28; 1 Corinthians 13:4-8; Romans 14:19; 15:2.

NO MORE TO WONDER

O city of Jerusalem,
How often would I;
Have drawn in your children,
But you would not come nigh.
    Your Maker and Redeemer,
    Who called you into "Light";
    Though you were founded in "Peace,"
    You chose a bloody plight.
The "Cornerstone" rejected,
Has come the "Main Support";
Of Jesus' Holy temple,
To those who call Him Lord!
    Gentiles, see that God's with you,
    Why don't you realize?
    All prophecies were fulfilled,
    Before your darkened eyes.
Wash your hearts from wickedness,
Accept Yeshua now;
O break up that fallow ground,
And let "Him" work to plow.
    The "Seed" of Life Eternal,
    That Jesus procreates;
    And bring you to His Presence,
    With His Life you're innate!
All God asks is devotion,
And your obedience;
To believe in "That Seed,"
Was Jesus Whom He sent!
    Messiah's Second Coming,
    Will be no more to save;
    But judgment and His wrath,
    Revealed on that "Great Day"!

O comfort ye my people,
This "sacrifice" is free;
For that "war" within your soul,
To finally be "Peace."

1 Corinthians 3:16; Hebrews 3:6; Zechariah 6:12-13; 7:14; 9:9; 12:10-14; 13:1,5-7;

Jeremiah 3:15; 17; 4:3-4; 14; 10:21; 23; Zephaniah 1:7; Matthew 21:42; 23:37;

II Corinthians 3:14; 6:16; 1 Peter 1:23; 2:4-5.

TRUE MAVERICKS!
BREAK THE HOARDING HERD!

You hold and squeeze and with all your might,
The compromise and think you're right.
With fists fastened, you hold so tight,
Though with this grip, it still takes flight!
 For what you hoard, you soon will lose,
 So, don't blame God when you're confused.
 God said to give and we'll receive,
 But selfishness cannot conceive.
Your storehouses filled with plenty,
And the "Word" spread as we ante.
Into the game of life we play,
With God's rules we look to pray.
 And seek the Lord as how to give,
 'Cause prosperity is to live.
 To bless and share this Gospel of
 How God first gave to us "His Love."
In Jesus Who has died for all,
And lifted us from that "Great Fall"!
He puts an end to greed and lust,
Oh, see how Jesus redeemed us!
 From sickness, poverty, and sin,
 By being cursed, doomed and beaten.
 The law of death we once were bound,
 Though now, through Christ, we can be found.
Receiving life, joy, peace and health,
All these He gives to us and wealth.
No man is justified by Law,
But through His Grace given to all.
 Those that believe, trust, and rely,
 Oh Jesus Christ, He Son Who died.
 It's man's nature to rob and steal,
 Yet God's is that to love and heal!

Are we so foolish not to see,
That bondage can never free?
For what you have will be required,
So see God's will as your desire.
Lend to the Lord and Bless the poor,
And keep a hospitable door.
Into your heart and save the Lost,
To share "His Love" at any cost!
Oh, be not weary in doing,
'Cause He rewards us as we bring.
Those into His Kingdom each week,
And being strong with Spirit meek.
Then we'll rejoice in one accord,
While hearing, "Come up" from our Lord!

Galatians 3; Luke 6:37-38; 14:14; II Corinthians 9:6-11; Ephesians 3:19-21; 6:18;

4:18-19; Philippians 4:8-9, 13, 19; Malachi 3:10; Exodus 23:25; Matthew 6:33;

Psalm 107:9-13; 1 Thessalonians 3:11-13; Proverbs 11:12, 27-31; 22:4, 9; 23:7;

II Thessalonians 3:13; Isaiah 3:10.

LET HIM WHO PRAYS, PRAISE!

From the rising of the sun,
'Till setting of the same;
The precious saints of our Lord,
Give glory to His Name!
    None is like the Lord our God,
    Who has His seat on high;
    Humbling Himself to regard,
    The earth and Heaven's sky!
Raising the poor out of dust,
The humble He'll exalt;
And the "*barren women,*"
His endless grace is brought.
    To make a joyful "*mother,*"
    That keeps a happy home;
    Who prays with praise her children,
    The Lord they'll make their own!
God so loves the unity,
A family will bring;
As they worship and observe,
Their Lord and King of Kings!
    This "family's" built of love,
    Not one that's recruited;
    With a "power" to strengthen,
    All righteousness imputed!
Oh! Thou are truly worthy,
To receive our praise;
All glory, power and honor,
It's "Your Name" that we raise.
    With greatest exaltation,
    In one accord we sing;
    And magnify "Him" Who died,
    Salvation's note to "ring!"

Psalm 113; 107:41-43; 57:7-11; 47:9; Romans 4:22-25; 10:13; John 14:13; Philippians

2:9-10; Ephesians 4:14-18; 1 Peter 5:6; Jude 20-25; Revelation 7:12; 5:9; 19:1, 16.

A NEW DAY DAWNS

Michael, those days have finally come,
When school and classes are now done.
You've hung in there and I'm so proud,
To see you rise and reach that cloud.

    To which "achievers" only hover,
    Then climb new heights to discover!
    My prayers for you to continue,
    Are enriched to know what's in you.

For discipline you have maintained,
And "trust in God" to please His aim!
You have worked hard and will receive,
Yet "hold on" to what you believe.

    See first the Kingdom of our Lord,
    And "He'll" reward you even more!
    God bless you on your launch in life,
    And may His Love keep your days bright!

Praise God! You did it!

DEAR JESUS,

I love You, Jesus, and thank You
For being my Lord of all I do.
My Savior, Healer, Son of God,
Prince of Peace, and my Advocate.
    My Intercessor and my Joy,
    My Baptizer in the Holy Ghost;
    My Counselor and my Friend;
    Elder Brother to me, Redeemed.
You're my High Priest and Present Help
In time of need. You give me wealth;
My Victory and my Strength,
My Wisdom and soon-coming King.
    The mighty God and Word made flesh;
    My Burden Bearer and Righteousness.
    God's First Born up from the dead,
    By whose Spirit I'm now led;
The cornerstone of my Spirit,
All things of Yours I inherit!

DEAR HOLY SPIRIT,

Praise you, Holy Ghost, for being
My Guide and Love in me living.
My Power and my Comforter;
Word Teacher and my Prayer Partner.
    Revealer of God's Truth and Rest,
    You're my Perfector and Boldness.
    My Gift Giver to speak a Word,
    Of Wisdom and Knowledge I've heard.
The One who gives me prophecy,
To interpret God's divine things.
The One whose purpose is made known,
As I speak to my God in tongues.
    Discerner of Spirit who's All Truth,
    The One that grows in me these fruits.
    Of Love, Joy, Peace and Patience,
    Self-control and faithfulness.
Sanctifier within me,
Who keeps me to live holy!

DEAR GOD,

I love You, Father, and give thanks,
For being my All and my Strength.
The Inhabitor of my Praise,
And Establisher of my ways.
   My Eternal God and Maker,
   Of me and of the Universe.
   Protector of my life and King,
   Giver of all Grace and Blessing.
My Love who is Love and my Light,
My Banner who sees through the night.
My Praise and Worship, the Almighty,
Lord God of Earth and the Heavenly.
   Resister of the proud who part,
   Exaltor of the meek in heart.
   You're my Provider and my Peace,
   And All Sufficient for my needs.
My Deliverer and my Help,
You create the fruit of my lips.
Oh, Praise You for all your Greatness,

All Merciful in whom I'm Blessed!

Psalm 69:30; Jeremiah 30:19; Psalm 103:1-2.

HOMOLETICS

"Daddy, daddy, where are you?"
The thought often came to mind.
"I'm in the den, what do you need?"
What I need dad is your time!
    The closeness of a family
    Is far from what used to be
    Though my mom was usually home
    My dad seemed aloof to me.
One night while camping with a boy scout friend,
When I was only twelve,
I was asked to do something that aroused me
And melted my morals as well.
    My innocence was taken
    But curiosity gave it up
    Now "Guy" was moving to Texas
    Like nothing happened, it ended abrupt.
A fire burned in my loins
To try this once again
Then conveniently it seemed to me
I met another friend.
    He thought I's cool plus I had a car
    Let's sneak off and drink some beer
    When high and look'n for girls had failed
    I began with Larry to engineer.
How devious the mind can be
When our flesh wants its' way
Now Larry was my second lover
As sexually we learned to play.
    My parents knew that I acted weird,
    They thought it would somehow pass.
    Then sixteen came and I didn't change
    But grew worse while smoking grass.

You'll not do that and live in our house
Was made to me very clear.
The hidden thoughts that came across was:
"We are ashamed of you because you are queer."
    But I really wasn't, it just filled a need
    When the girls I asked didn't go out
    But it tore my mom and my dad gave up
    As they couldn't figure what I was about.
I was raised in church all my life
Yet intrigue out weighed conviction
How could a "loving" God nuke the Sodomites
Was my confused benediction.
    Senior year of seventy-two
    A chance to play college ball
    A reachable dream 'cause I was so mean
    Was thwarted from "drinking" that Fall.
In trouble with the law I ran
And hitch hiked out to L.A.
Where I learned that mom protracted cancer
My heart told me I had debts to pay.
    Never underestimate
    The prayers of a Grandma
    While I still had to make the choice
    To obey God and man's law.
It was a relationship with a Pastor
Who bailed me out of jail
That set my heart on "Heaven's Gift"
Instead of those who bent toward hell.
    No, it was not immediate
    But progressively I grew
    Even "smoked up" going to Bible class
    God's love radiantly shone through.
It seems most creative people
Are always on Satan's hit list

I implore you, "Give it to God!"
And let your gifted talents find bliss.
    Five times I've nearly died
    From drugs, car wrecks or fire
    Yet by God's Grace I've lived to tell
    And hopefully inspire:
That it's this Father's love that changed my life
As I received His Son.
He's cleansed my sins and forgiven me
To accomplish what "I" couldn't get done.
    Temptations still come to harass
    But it's God's strength and not that if mine.
    Please accept Jesus' love for you
    Because there is "No" guarantee of more time.

Signed,
From many who hurt and want help!

MY SUN, SA LANG' HAB NI DA

(I Love You)

Sun, you shine a light in me
That warms my every bone
Penetrating to my heart
A love whose place is home!
    Inspired, not tired, though being alone
    For soon, you'll stay with me
    Seeing our lives combined to thrive
    As "one" to grow and breed:
Seeds of Joy which sprout desires
We graciously release
Seeking His presence always
That fills our family's peace!
    It's true, I may not know you much,
    But God's known all along
    How to compliment our lives
    And make our link real strong.
Gentle are your ways dear Sun,
Of which, I need to learn:
How rough edges can be smoothed
While character stays firm!
    May I be security
    With God's hand to uphold
    Your life with mine so we will find
    Our visions to unfold.
And be a living witness
Of "LOVE" who joined us both
Committing to the "Same"
Our solemn marriage oath!

I Love you, Sun Kim!

"BREAKING THE BREAD"

Jesus said to feed my sheep
And made no reservations
Toward how we felt or what we thought
But kept His firm confession!
 Oh Lord, our works are many
 And Don't you realize:
 The law we've kept, though times inept,
 Oh, can't you hear our cries?
Then Jesus quotes His Word to us
My children know it's Me
You give to those with hands held out
And fill their waning needs!
 AWAKE! Ye slumbering giant
 And storm the gates of hell,
 Breaking loose those chains which bind
 Freeing all that we tell:
Peace we give as He has given
With Love to mend the souls
Oh stand My Holy Ground
And "hear," I give control:
 To those who trust, love, and obey
 The unction of my Spirit
 "Doing" what I've called them to
 Not "passive," who only hear it!
Your cries must come from inside
Not whimpering welps of help
Yet rather Righteous prayers of faith
Feeling as I felt:
 When multitudes would cling to Me
 Aware of just My Name
 Which now endorses all of you.
 Who'll glory not in "their" fame,

But in the riches of my might
Testifying amidst the fight:
Greater is He who is in me
Because my Lord is victory!
   The battles won have not all shown
   The intensity of what's begun
   For in My Grace, I've picked you out
   And you chose to use My clout!
The land my friends I've given thee
To Redeem those lost back to me!

LIVING BROOKS

God made me hope from mama's womb
"In thee," I shall depend
Upon her breast, I'm refreshed,
But God's my start and end!
    God fulfilled our petition
    For we regard your Name
    Giving us a healthy baby
    Where he may serve the "Same."
The Lord has built this house
Our labor's not in vain,
Likewise, our child's heritage
Is blessed and will remain!
    Thank you Lord for your reward
    In this precious son
    Seeing our lives combine and thrive
    With you to be as one:
That can NOT tear by might of man
Nor demon thoughts of foe.
For we allow your Spirit's peace;
"Surround us, Sweep us, Flow!
    Jonathan Ryan, you're a prophet
    Called forth from mother's womb
    And you indeed shall succeed
    To be trained and well groomed…
With wisdom, power, might and love
Discretion you've obtained
Loathing sin and evil,
As Your Father does, you disdain!
    Forever is Your Mercy Lord
    And Your Righteousness
    For our children to continue
    That we be established.

Oh strength and praises of our Lord
Greatly be revealed
To our child as we incline
Our ears to hear your will!
    We choose life, for our seed,
    Is blessed with NO sickness
    Nor any plague shall come their way
    To become a hindrance.
As heaven and earth praise the Lord,
And all that is within it,
So the see that love His name
Their Praise shall He inhabit!

I love you Jonathan Ryan!

Isaiah 54:13; Proverbs 2:6; 22:6; Isaiah 49:25; Ephesians 6:4; Proverbs 29:17; 13:1, 24;

Genesis 15:5; Deuteronomy 30:19; 33:19; 28—all, 7:12-15; Psalm 91—all; 112:1-5; 69:34-36;

103:17; 78:4; 102:28; 128:3; 1 Timothy 2:15.

"THE YELLOW ROSE FROM TEXAS"

She's the yellow rose from Texas
Who has meant the world to me
She brought me into this earth
A life lived happily
    Through the pain I felt when Ruth, my dog,
    Left this boy of twelve
    She stood there by my side with love
    And gentleness to help!
No defense lawyer could have
Rent a better case
Yet all the while, she hoped in me
I'd learn from my mistakes.
    I could not ever lie to her
    Cause she'd know before I said it
    So a screen of silence rose
    But melted when her love hit!
Expelled while in the 4th grade
And really quite confused
Mother too was frustrated
Though couldn't help but muse:
    "This child is driving me crazy!"
    "Why should I ever try?"
    Then a tear thought from her parent's years
    Made her sign then cry:
"A family's bond cannot just be
Held firm while things only run smooth
But giving grace a little space
To cover that we don't always approve!
    When love's the main ingredient
    You fill into your child's life,
    Expect success to come from them
    Their days to shine so bright!

What more could be said of this rose
For perennially it blooms
In each precious bud she bore
Petals of love were groomed!

I Love you Mom!

FORTY-FIED SISTER

Have your 40 years in the wilderness
Seemed trite and without cause?
Or are the standing O's still to come
With uncontrollable applause?
    Could the tornado hitting Sheppard Hospital
    Been a precursor of storms to follow?
    My, how the turbulent winds that molds us
    Are often hard to swallow.
A constant figure in my life
You've helped me when I was down
You're not much of a complainer
Nor one to frame a frown.
    You'll always be the prom queen
    That I's proud to be my sister
    But the salient point I consider of you
    Is your willingness to be a good listener,
Four decades haven't found you Deb
I pray they never will
Please keep your upbeat attitude
Toward others you instill.
    A bed of roses we weren't promised
    But if we were, you'd be
    The prettiest one ever planted
    Glowing in aesthetic beauty.
God keep you strong in health and hope
Endearing every moment
As time thoughtful of our Maker makes
Us grateful of Jesus' atonement.

God Bless You, Deb!

"CONQUERING CANCER"

I know your oft' impatience
Those grueling test you do
But oh, the character you've shown
Courageously making it through.
    I'm glad to see this winding down
    And Pray "it" never returns
    'Cause seeing you healthy and full of life
    Is always our main concern.
Mom, you've been so special
A sharer with our woes,
At times they were just laid on you;
Others because you chose...
    To give us of your wisdom,
    Instructions, and advice.
    Even admist stubborn response
    Your candor remained nice.
Thank you for keeping the boys,
A Herculon feat at best,
Thanks for inviting us in
When you really needed rest.
    We love you Mom and pray your dreams
    Totally come true
    For no one is near as worthy
    Nor beautiful a person as you!

IN MEMORY OF RONNIE HOUSTON

Swaying on a mountain swing
Or head first down the slide
Never really serious
Yet one you could confide.
    Ronnie Houston was a playful sort
    And fun to be around
    His energy would let you see
    A smile that couldn't frown.
Why should a young man in his prime
So tragically go?
Why should a mother hold such grief?
There's much I'd like to know.
    Those ravages that satan plays,
    Upon the ones we love,
    Are kept in check, lest we e'er neglect,
    God's power from above.
Memories though, can't be robbed
Especially those that Ronnie brought
A friend I knew as a child
We romped and played, oh, so wild.
    Picnics, swimming, and fishing holes
    A grateful life he led
    Now Beth is left to pick up
    Those moments with him that fled…
As a vapor, back to its cloud
We too, shall rise one day,
If that dew that's a part of you,
Is Jesus all the way…
    Through the valley who's shadow is death
    And even on our peaks
    By the one who heals sad hearts
    And strengthens those who're weak!

He said, "I'll never leave you,
Yet your home I must prepare,
And yes, I know your son's loss hurts,
But believe Me, I do care!"
    This earth is moaning just as you
    Knowing her time is short
    For globally God's trumpet call
    Shall be for us, "Report!"
Ronnie's seed shall carry on
In attributes my Son has shown.
Hold fast to your faith in Jesus Christ
And grasp for that water of Eternal Life!

"CAN YOU SEE BEYOND MY LIMP?"

An athletic jock for most of my life
Up until a few years ago
Then Father Time and injuries
Caught up to make my body slow.
    At times frustration overwhelms me
    I need the fire of desire to kick in
    So workouts at the gym and hiking
    Receives all that I have of adrenaline
A firefighter for 17 years
I experienced other's pain and loss
But for God's Grace in my own life
I wouldn't struggle to pay the cost...
    To be a servant who doesn't complain
    Faithful to fulfill God's Way
    Although "often" I've offered Him my own ideas
    And even sidetrack them and stray.
Jacob wrestled with God for his blessing
And wound up with his hip out and a limp
But just because we wrestle with God's will for us
Doesn't mean we can't handle it or we are a wimp.
    A good man's steps are ordered by the Lord
    And I'm trying to not walk out of line
    At least if I stay in the right direction
    I hope He'll allow me more time...
To find the destiny He has for me
And continue to bless those in need
For now my trials are just part of life
And I may limp into Glory but it will be without strife.

"LITTLE SISTER DON'T YOU RUN"

Little sister don't you run
Away from time and love
One ends but not the other.
Now you're watching from above.
    A bruised yet still lovely flower
    That blossomed early for all to gaze.
    I wished she had weathered the storm of life better
    Instead of getting lost in its trouble and maze.
Even the most delicate and sensitive flowers
Need the warmth of the "Son" to exist
Especially when bad soil clings to foil
Your roots so you must shake loose and resist.
    I pray in time some solace we'll find
    As to why Laurie didn't finish her race
    But to honor her we must all keep running
    With endurance through hardships we face.
Many times my life's baton I've wanted to hand off
Or for that matter chuck it into the stands
Even though I'm a fierce competitor
How can a slow runner keep pace with such demands?
    The Author and Finisher or out faith
    Neither sleeps nor does He slumber
    And when we stray off from the course
    Our steps He'll correct from our blunder.
I feel Laurie's skills from nursing may now serve her
As she ministers to babies in Heaven
And there will be peace with no sorrow but joy
In this realm of God's dimension.
    May those memories shine bright of Laurie
    In a reflection from her beautiful smile.
    When our own contests are challenged with cramps and sore muscles
    Let us grab her baton and by God's Grace finish that extra mile.

I love you sis',
Joel William Addison

Romans 14:19; 15:2; 1 Thessalonians 5:11—Let us aim or and eagerly pursue and practice what makes for peace by edifying, admonishing, encouraging, and strengthening one another in the Bond of Love through Jesus Christ, our Mediator, that we might bring others into harmony with Him.

Psalm 86:10-12—For You are great and work wonders! You alone are God! Teach me Your Way, O Lord, that I may walk and live in Your truth; direct and unite my heart to reverence and honor Your name. I will confess and praise You, O Lord my God, with my whole heart; and I will glorify Your name forevermore!

Proverbs 16:24—Pleasant words are as an honeycomb, sweet to the soul and health to the bones.

FIVE STEPS TO EVANGELISM

Read Acts 10:33-48.

The five steps are pray, praise, teach, preach, then practice healing and deliverance with signs and wonders confirming your witness and God's Word you've presented.

PRAY: As in verse 33, these people were ready, we too must intercede for he lost and be ready. (Note: God will not do a thing before it's revealed to His prophets so the preparation can be laid out. God is a God of order, just as a football game has both sides ready to go at the whistle, or trumpet in our case, either way there's a signal. That's why when you walk in the Spirit, you'll NOT fulfill the lust of the flesh. When you're in tune with the voice of Jesus, His words anoint the airwaves and get that carnal mind off yourself and tuned to others.)

a. Peter was willing to be willing, but not real discerning, but after three visions, the Spirit of God directly telling him, and angels going out from his prayer to bring contact with Cornelius to him, he finally got the revelation: "I'm the one," but still when he got there, asked them, "What is the cause for you to have me come?" (Note: The words angel is messenger, so, do you get the message?)

b. The harvest is always plenteous though the laborers are few. Then it says, "Pray ye the Lord of the harvest to SEND laborers." (Note: The angels gather the final harvest among the tares and the wheat, so since they are sent to minister to those called of God, we can expect the same results as we go out into our Jerusalem or Marietta to proclaim the Gospel of Jesus! When we truly are willing, we will sense, by the Spirit, the urgency of the hour and the wave of God's Power He desires us to ride on.

c. Just as He heard Israel in Egypt, God hears the cries of His people, but still channels His power through us like where Jesus said, "All power and authority is given unto thee in heaven and earth and I have the keys of the Kingdom. NOW I'm delegating you to go in the power of My Spirit and whatever you bind on earth, My Father's already bound in heaven and whatever you loose upon earth, it's loosed in heaven, so bind the principalities, powers and rulers of darkness of apathy, fear, doubt, strife, lust, confusion and all that should come against you and those you're going forth to minister My life to."

Using the spiritual weaponry I've given you through the holy, impregnable name of My Son Jesus, which is above all names, now loose those children of darkness to enter My Kingdom of Light, for they are drawn by My Spirit in you, but you must make the first step to go willingly and I'll be with you.

Loose the gifts and fruit of the Spirit to operate in your behalf for they go hand in hand. (1) Words of wisdom in love; (2) Words of knowledge with joy; (3) Gift of faith peaceably; (4) Healing with My longsuffering; (5) Miracles in a gentle humble spirit; (6) Prophecy with all goodness to edify; (7) Discerning of spirits by the faithfulness of the Holy Ghost to bear witness to the truth and (8) Tongues with temperance being thoughtful of others and its need. (9)Interpretation of tongues with self-control knowing that the Holy Spirit is interpreting not you. (Note: Blessed are they that do the will of their Father.)

d. Those things you've prayed for, believe you've received them and call those aimless children found and directed by God and His angels to come before your paths and that you are spiritually perceptive of their needs and hunger for the truth which will set them free!

2. PRAISE God for the souls won over to Him and the victory He's already declared we have, for God causes us to triumph in all things and that no evil shall befall us not any plague come nigh over dwellings, and that every tongue that should rise against use, we shall judge, SILENT! Praise Him in Spirit and in truth by the Spirit of truth in confirming with our spirits the validity to where our maneuvers will occur, thus not

allowing any time for Satan to even instigate roadblocks. (Note: As you go out, be sure to get contact with the window of their souls: the eyes. Then speak the truth in love whereby the entrance of God's Word in you to them will bring light, thus letting your light so shine before men as a witness unto Jesus!)

3. TEACH: Verse 34—Peter showed the love of God knows not bounds and the doors to the Kingdom are open to whosoever will, for God is not respecter of persons and Jesus died for all.

a. Proclaim the peace God wants His man to live in and by relation to Him through Jesus is the only means to obtain such peace.

Note: Make your presentation in this manner of gentleness and quiet assurance of Whom you serve!

b. Emphatically, not desperately, convey that Jesus must be received, believed on, and trusted as the Lord of their life with all their heart and not just mental assent.

4. PREACH: That Jesus dies that we might live; suffered so we could be relieved; became poor that we would be rich; bore sickness so we could be healed; received abuse, scorn and rejection to remedy our pain in these areas; and was tempted in all things to forsake God and His call for Him so as to give us a victory over ANY lust or temptation.

a. All these are contingent on OUR choice like in Deuteronomy 30:19, where God calls a record to be made in heaven and earth that He sets before you life and death or a blessing and a curse, then appeals to you to "choose life" but the decision rests upon you.

b. Hear the person out, be compassionate, say the Word of Reconciliation that their sins are forgiven and God loves them and wants them born anew unto Him so to fellowship, answer their prayers, build them up, be encouragement and strength to them; make their life worthwhile and heal their family and problems.

5. Through the practice or application of the words Jesus instructed us in Mark 16: 15-18; to proclaim this Good News to the world expectantly, ready to drive out demons, oppression, or Satan himself if he gets in the way, plus attacking him and his agents with a code language, commonly known as new tongues, to surround his flanks with armaments which shall destroy his works of sickness, disease, poverty, famine, greed and idolatry whereby the Church, Christ's Body, when realizing this and acting on it, makes the light of Jesus in us, to shatter the darkness and the gates if hell to not prevail against our charge.

The sick shall be healed, the captives freed, the blind to see, with praise and worship aroused from the signs and wonders following to confirm the Word and ushering our Lord and Savior Jesus as in Acts 3:19—21, we, Jesus' body make. Acts 2:34-35: His enemies His footstool and announcing the era for total recovery to come.

IN CHRIST...

My Confessions are:

II Corinthians 5:17—I am in Christ, I am a new creature: old things have passed away and all things have become new.

Ephesians 1:7-8—In Jesus I have redemption through His blood, the forgiveness of sins, according to the riches of his grace; Wherein He hath abounded me to all wisdom and prudence.

Acts 17:28—For in Jesus I live, and move, and have my being.

Colossians 1:13—In Christ, God has delivered me from the power of darkness, and has translated me into the Kingdom of His dear Son, therefore Satan has no power or authority in my life...

1 John 4:4—I am of God and have overcome them: because greater is He that is in me than he that is in the world.

Isaiah 41:10—I will not fear; for God is with me and I shall not be dismayed; for Jehovah is my God and will strengthen me, help me, and uphold me with the right hand of His righteousness.

Romans 8:31—Thank God, for he is in me and if God be for me, no one can be against me. Praise the Lord!

Philippians 4:19—My God shall supply all of my needs according to His riches in glory by Christ Jesus.

Philippians 4:13—I can do all things through Christ which strengthens me. (The joy of the Lord is my strength, therefore, I shall please and praise Him and do all things to the glory of his name.)

Luke 1:37—For with God, nothing shall be impossible for me.

Isaiah 54:17—No weapon that is formed against me shall prosper; and every tongue that shall rise against me, in judgment, it shall be silenced. This is the heritage of the servants of the Lord, and my righteousness is of Jesus!

The Lord is going before me, the blood of Jesus is over me, the everlasting arms of my Father God are under me, and surely goodness and mercy are behind me, following all the days of my life!

Deuteronomy 8: 18—I remember the Lord my God in tithes and offerings; for it is He that gives me power to get wealth, that He may establish He covenant and I may bless others.

Joshua 1:8; James 1:19—I Speak, think, seek, and act on God's word and I am slow to wrath, quick to forgive, instant in prayer and I prosper and have good success wherever I go.

1 John 3:21-22; John 5:15; Mark 11:24—I do keep God's commandments and do those things pleasing in His sight and I am confident that as I ask anything according to his Word, He hears me and I believe I receive the petition I desire of Him.

I am redeemed from the curse of the law for Jesus Christ is my redeemer and because Christ bore my sicknesses and diseases and suffered those torturous stripes for my healing, I am right now! In divine health, immune to disease, healed of anything Satan's got to try and put on me. I'm walking in spiritual and physical prosperity. Praise God!

Deuteronomy 28: 1-14

MY CONFESSION OF LOVE

Father, in the name of Jesus, reveal to my spirit man the reality of walking in Your love. Create the image within me of Your love that fulfills all the law.

By faith I commit myself to receive and act on the revelation of God's love in my heart. I make it my quest always. I will meditate in Your Word and ponder and study the love of God to the point that it governs my thinking, my speech, and my actions. I receive it done in me now and continually as I pray and praise You for it. In Jesus' name. Amen.

1 Corinthians 3:16—My body is the temple of God and the Holy Spirit dwells in me and I shall not defile my body no that of others.

Ephesians 6:10—I am strong in the Lord and in the power of His might.

Ephesians 3:12—In Jesus I have boldness and access with confidence to God my Father by the faith of Him.

Colossians 2: 6-7—I have received Christ Jesus my Lord, and I walk in Him, being rooted and built up in Him and established in the faith through His Word abounding always with thanksgiving for it.

Father, I am praying according to your Word (Matthew 16:19), that You send forth my angels and free my family from the spirits of fear, doubt, confusion, and religious tradition and that those evil spirits be bound and never rise up in me nor my family, in Jesus' name.

Philippians1:14—I stand confident in the Lord and in the power of His grace toward me a believer and I grow bolder and bolder to speak His Word without fear.

Father, as I speak the truth in love, may my family receive it gladly. May they ever search the Scriptures and study the Word to show themselves approved unto You, O God! Open the eyes of their understanding and enlighten their spirits to the truth. Give them a spirit of power and love and of a sound mind.

Hebrews 4:16—I come boldly, not arrogantly, into the throne of grace with my prayers to God. Through Jesus Christ, Amen.

Luke 24:49—I'm endued with power from on high.

Acts 4:31—I'm filled with the Holy Ghost and speak the Word of God with boldness.

II Corinthians 7:4; Hebrews 13:6—Great is my boldness of speech, for the Lord is my helper and I will not fear what man shall do to me.

Titus 2:14; 3:8; Hebrews 10:24; James 2:17; Romans 5:1; Galatians 5:6—I'm zealous to constantly maintain good works and be considerate of others, inspiring them unto love and good works, too. For faith, if it has not works, is dead, being alone. The just shall live by faith and faith worketh by love! In Jesus' Name.

The triumph I have in Christ is not that of just boisterous action for the Lord, but it's the triumph I have residing deep down in my soul and spirit thus releasing the assurance I have that God and His holy angels will back me as I go forth speaking and doing His Word and walking in His love. In Jesus' name.

Daniel 12:3—They that be wise shall shine as the brightness of the firmament and they that turn many to righteousness, as the stars forever.

Mark 16: 17-18—I'm a believer and these signs follow me: in Jesus' name I cast out devils, I speak with new tongues. If I take up serpents or drink any deadly thing unknowingly, it shall not hurt me. I lay hands on the sick and they shall recover. Through the life of God in me and the mighty name of Jesus, I bring deliverance to the captives and relief to the suffering. Jesus does the healing through me, for I'm but a vessel fit for the Master's use and I administer that mighty power under the authority in the name above all names—Jesus!

FULL OF FAITH!

II Chronicles 15:13—I'm entered into a covenant to seek the Lord god with all my heart and soul! In Jesus' Name!

Psalm 31:23; 101:6—The Lord preserves me for I'm faithful to Him and His Word. His eyes are upon me always.

Proverbs 28:20—Being faithful, I abound with blessings.

Matthew 25:21—I'm faithful over few and many things.

II Thessalonians 3:3—The Lord is faithful who establishes me!

II Timothy 6:2—I give honor and service to those who are over me and in like manner it is returned to me.

Jeremiah 18:28; III John 5—I speak God's Word and whatever I do, I do it faithfully as unto my Lord Jesus.

FAVOR

Genesis 18:3—As Abraham, I've obtained favor of my Father God, plus a better covenant and greater promises.

Psalm 112: 1-5—Praise the Lord! I am in awe of God and I greatly delight to do His commandments. My seed and generations are blessed. Wealth and riches are in my house and my love endures forever. I'm upright in my heart and God's glory lights my path as my steps are ordered of Him. I am gracious, full of compassion and righteousness. I'm a good man, lover of Jesus, doer of His Words and a giver well able to lend and bless others.

Romans 8:14; Luke 1:30; 2:52—I've found favor with God and man. I am led and constantly walk by the Holy Spirit and am given the ability to gain wealth, finance the Gospel and meet needs of others.

Isaiah 48: 17, 15—The Lord, my redeemer, the Holy One of Israel, my God, teaches me to profit and leads me in the way that I should go. And through heeding the voice of the good shepherd, He establishes me and I make my way prosperous.

John 10:3; Exodus 12:26; II Peter 1:1-4; Philippians 4:19; I Peter 4:10, Deuteronomy 28; Malachi 3:10; Luke 16:2; Psalm 1:2-3—As God has given me favor with Him and man, plus all things that pertain to life and godliness, my needs are met according to "His riches" in glory by Christ Jesus, and I apply this in meditating day and night in His Word to observe and do those things that are written therein that my "light" might so shine before men and glorify my Father, being a witness unto Jesus bearing much good fruit, and being a wise steward, faithful and prudent over all God has entrusted into my care. Whatever I do prospers and I have good success. God will give me all grace and glory and withholds no good thing from me and He rebukes Satan for me and pours His blessings on me.

GOD'S ANSWER TO FAT: LOSE IT

Proverbs 23:2—Put a knife to your throat if you're given to overeat. Therefore my confession is: I'm not given to gluttony and I refrain from sweets and dainties for they are a deceitful meat and Satan works through deception, but I am aware of his wiley schemes for I have the wisdom and mind of Christ.

Ecclesiastes 6:7; Luke 4:4—All the labor of man is for his mouth and yet his appetite is not filled. Therefore I labor for the Lord because man does not live by bread alone, but by every word of God. In Jesus' name I claim this.

I Corinthians 9:27; Ephesians 5:26—I keep my body under subjection lest by any mean when I preach to others I myself should be taken lightly in not doing the Word. I eat properly and proportionally, not given to fatty foods nor those that would defile my body, plus I discipline my body and its members to consistent exercise and sleep, and I renew my mind daily and cleanse it by the washing of regeneration by the Word. I'm instant in prayer and I praise God for a perfect body, perfect health and perfect obedience to Him in the name of Jesus.

Proverbs 25:16—Hast thou found honey? Eat so much as is sufficient for thee lest thou be filled therewith and vomit it. (I eat only what I need and I don't desire any more in Jesus' Name.)

Numbers 11: 32-34—I realize as Israel gluttonized on the quails and did sin and provoked God's wrath to where, out of their disobedience, they also gave place to the devil and he cursed them with a great plague; thus when you get out of the will or Word of God, you are open game for Satan. Right now, I rebuke Satan and the spirit of gluttony and ever hold fast to the fact that my body is the temple of the Holy Ghost, which I will never defile. In Jesus' name.

II Peter 1:5—I diligently seek to add to my faith, virtue; and to my virtue, knowledge; and to my knowledge, self-control; and to my self-control, patience. And to my patience, godliness, and to my godliness, brotherly kindness; and to my brotherly kindness, love. Praise God! Father, I desire to walk in Your love and I do refuse to overeat. In Jesus' Name.

UNITY OF OUR FAITH
IN PRAYER AND PRAISE

The walls shaken when we get in one accord and pray for one another are "Spiritual strongholds" which have been built up to block us from fulfilling God's commission for our lives. (Note: It was praise that crumbled the walls of Jericho.) Also the walls to the gates of hell shall not prevail against our onslaught of united prayer and praise that gathers "His strength" collectively in each believer thus, not being of our might nor power, but by His Spirit which inhabits our praise. In that atmosphere, the enemy is stilled and silenced because "his" gates are blown open, his walls are shaking, and with God in the middle of the scene, their so-called fearless leader, the devil, is fleeing in stark terror. Wake up, Church!

God ordained praise for this purpose and it leaves with it the result of taking back what Jesus redeemed, namely; mankind; all things pertaining to life and godliness; divine health; and wealth laid up for the righteous called of God Who says, "It's yours; I've given you the keys of this Kingdom so you have the right to bind or loose whatever you will in the authority anything by those united prayers so I can give it to you."

Examples: Your new building to train and reinforce My army; your city; your witnessing unto Me; and your bearing much good fruit to glorify Me! Don't relent! Pray for one another that ye may be healed, give of yourself to others so I may see it being bountifully given unto you. This is a mandate! Impel My people to come together and bask in this harmony so they are sensitive to those in need whereby they may sow their "talents" of love, time, wisdom, and monetary goods. As they present these and their increase, I am obligated to and delightful of the "fact" that I can NOW watch over My Word they've done to perform it in blessing My people with the storehouses of heaven immeasurably prepared for them, plus exalting them in their position of life so they can do more for My gifts bestowed for My calling in you are not repented of nor turned away but purposed to allow you grace and mercy in time of need; supernatural faith for those ignorant of My Word, and the whole redemptive plan of Jesus dying to get My children, who were kidnapped and held at ransom from

Adam till then! The plan worked and Jesus ever lives and intercedes to see it carried out, but depends on His ambassadors to lay claim to each of My redeemed purchases by convincing them. "They are free" by the Blood of the Lamb and the Word of god in their testifying to the acceptance of Jesus as the Lord of their life with complete trust and reliance in Him, Satan cannot keep My sheep from walking out of his domain once they've heard the truth, the way, and the life: Jesus! I've called them delivered from the foundation of the world, so you do likewise.

EXAMPLES OF KNOWING GOD

1. Knowing your wife—you will:
Bless, encourage, and speak well of & to your wife giving praise for them and showing your appreciation creatively.
a. Do we do this to the "Lover" of our life or tell others of such relationship to the One who IS LOVE?
Edify your wife and build up her self image and esteem. Acknowledge her accomplishments and dreams then develop a good prayer life praying God's richest blessings, health, peace, & fullness of Joy be upon her and stand in the gap protecting her with your own life & bind any fears from her.
b. Is this the attitude we hold towards God's "body" and His "members"?
Share time with your wife intimately. Rethink your priorities, talk and listen to "her" ideas, fears, and desires. (Note: When praying for my future wife I asked, "What can I do for you or give you that would please you most?" Well, I literally heard her voice say, "I want to be felt." Now, you can take that statement a number of ways but this should summize our own recognition of who she is and her purpose, as too, our feelings toward God.)
Touch, caress, and pet being mutually initiated and not all sexual.

2. Know—Talk intelligently with openness to learn.
a. earnest eye opening; awareness; discern and desire with violent passion; reaching forth mentally excited.
b. Old Testament—familiar friend, regard, respect, "understand"; care for, (same word—where Adam knew Eve), look intently with recognition, revere, perceive.
3. Isaiah 58:2; Psalm 9:10, Psalm 46:10—As we seek Him daily, we'll delight to know His ways recognizing the authority of His name with trust in Him thus being still and allowing God to be El Shaddi for all our needs. (Hosea 2:20; 6:3)
I will even betroth thee unto Me in faithfulness and thou shalt know the Lord and you shall know Him as My Holy Spirit's dawning brings the

heavy dew of Hermon by the latter and former rain springing up out of the earth of your soul overflowing to bless others and bare fruit like the Garden of Eden without works, per se, but in an intimate knowledge and relationship with Me as Adam & Enoch walked with Me and pleased Me in faith and trust for Me to provide but, (Hos 4:6) My people are destroyed for a lack of that same Knowledge & truth!

Put off the distractions of the world and know the Lord your God and My Son Jesus that we are one and desire that you be one and walk in love showing My Mercy and strength so I may show myself strong in your midst and inhabit your praise (2 Pet 3:18) and bask in My Grace growing in Knowledge and intimacy of My Word in you. (2 Pet 1:2-4) Let Grace and peace be multiplied through the knowledge of God and Jesus, Our Lord. According as His Divine power has given us all things that pertain unto Life and godliness through the knowledge of Him that called us to Glory & Virtue whereby are given unto us exceeding great and precious promises so by these we can partake of His Divine Love Nature having escaped the corruption in the world which comes through lust.

We are extensions of God's love, to the world and especially to our wives but He wants the connection made with Him first. This is so the riches of His goodness can be fully expressed and lead men to repentance and faith in a God and Savior who loves them and died for them!!

"THE SINNER'S PRAYER"

God, I confess that I'm a sinner in need of a Savior and worthy only of death but You sent Your only begotten Son, Jesus, to bear my sins on the cross at Calvary.

Dear God, forgive me for my sinful past living devoid of faith in you. I totally give you my life and devotion. Jesus, be my Lord and Savior. God, inhabit my spirit with your precious Holy Spirit. Save me, deliver me and heal me, Lord God. In the power and authority of Jesus' name, I ask You into my life.

THE WHITE HOUSE

WASHINGTON

November 22, 1985

Dear Mr. Addison:

You were good to think of Nancy and me and we
want you to know how pleased we are by your
kindness. Thank you for remembering us with
the inscribed copy of your collection of psalms
which you presented to Bob Sweet, Jr., during
a meeting at the White House. We truly appre-
ciate the support that prompted your spiritual
gift.

With our best wishes,

Sincerely,

Ronald Reagan

Mr. Joel Addison, Jr.
Apartment 17
1260 South Cobb Drive
Marietta, Georgia 30060

ABOUT THE AUTHOR:

Joel Addison was born on September 23, 1954 and has always had an affinity for nature. His mother and teachers said, "He sees things differently." As a young boy his grandfather, W.P. Addison, encouraged him to keep a record of his thoughts although, at the time, "wanting to play ball" seemed more important. After seeing the ease from which his poetry flowed off his pen and the pleasure it gave to his readers, he decided to pursue the gift whole heartedly.

Addison worked with the Smyrna Fire Dept for 17 years and has done electrical work since he was 12. In between the two for the past 25 years he has stayed "instant in season" to write as inspired to do so combining an earlier work with many newer poems since. From President Reagan's desk at the White House to the replaced walls at the Pentagon and across the ocean to China; Addison's poetry has traveled and longs to lodge in any heart that will hear!